Life Itself

To Peter Hayes,
a friend and a colleague,
with gratitude,
John Boe

Life Itself

Messiness Is Next to Goddessness and Other Essays

JOHN BOE

CHIRON PUBLICATIONS • WILMETTE, ILLINOIS

"Simeon, Apollo, and Dionysus: A Jungian Approach to the Mystery" originally appeared in *Murder Ink* (Workman, 1977). It is reprinted here with permission from Workman Publishing Co.

Lyrics from "I'll Never Be the Same," by Matt Melneck, Frank Signorelli, and Gus Kahn. © 1932 (copyright renewed 1960) c/o EMI ROBBINS CATALOG, INC. World rights controlled and administered by CCP/Belwin, Inc., Miami. Reprinted with permission of CPP/Belwin, Inc.

Photographs of the carvings by C. G. Jung, © 1993 by the Estate of C. G. Jung, are reproduced by permission of Niedieck Linder AG, Switzerland.

Jung, C. G., *Letters, Vol. 2 1951–1961.* © 1975 by Princeton University Press. Reprinted by permission of Princeton University Press.

Excerpt from *Tender Buttons* by Gertrude Stein is reprinted with permission from the Estate of Gertrude Stein.

"Messiness Is Next to Goddessness" (1992), "For Me and My Anima" (1989), "The Wolf in Jack London" (1980), and "The Introvert in Shakespeare" (1981) originally appeared in slightly different versions in *Psychological Perspectives*.

"Mistakes Were Made: Philosophy in an Off Key" (1987), "The Holidays of Darkness" (1987), "On My Back" (1988), and "A Time to Be Born" (1987) originally appeared in slightly different versions in the *East Bay Express*.

"Religion and Basketball" originally appeared in *Take It to the Hoop: A Basketball Anthology*, Daniel Rudman, ed. (North Atlantic Books, 1980).

"In the Palm of My Hand" (1988) originally appeared in the *Berkeley Monthly*.

"Don't Dream It, Be It: *The Rocky Horror Picture Show* as Dionysian Revel" (1983), "Marie-Louise von Franz and *The Way of the Dream*" (1986), and "Pleasing and Agreeable: An Interview with John Freeman" (1989) originally appeared in the *San Francisco Jung Institute Library Journal*.

"To Kill Mercutio: Thoughts on Shakespeare's Psychological Development" (1975) originally appeared in *Quadrant*.

"Notes: My Mother at the Piano" and "Life Itself" originally appeared in *Parents*, Ronald R. Geibert, ed. (Wright State University, Dayton Museum of Contemporary Art, 1992).

Library of Congress Catalog Card Number: 94-19711

Printed in the United States of America.
Editing and book design by Siobhan Drummond.
Cover design by D. J. Hyde.

Library of Congress Cataloging-in-Publication Data:
Boe, John, 1944–
Life itself : "Messiness is next to goddessness" and other essays / John Boe.
p. cm.
Essays, some rev., most previously published in various sources, 1975–1992.
Includes bibliographical references.
ISBN 0–933029–86–1 : $14.95
1. American wit and humor. 2. Boe, John, 1944– —Humor. I. Title
PN6162.B632 1994
814'.54 – dc20
94–19711
CIP

ISBN 0–933029–86–1

Cover: Painting by Margaret Boe Birns.

For my family

Contents

Acknowledgments

I MUST FIRST THANK the four people who have taught me the most about life: Carl Jung, William Shakespeare, Marie-Louise von Franz, and my mother Margaret Boe.

I want to thank the various editors who first published (and strove to improve) many of these pieces: John Beebe, Patrick Finley, Ronald Geibert, Rob Hurwitt, Ernest Lawrence Rossi, John Raeside, Daniel Rudman, Edward Gann Snyder, Pat and Becky Stone, William Walcott, and Dilys Winn, and also the various managing editors and copyeditors who have labored over my work. I give special thanks to my editor at Chiron, Murray Stein, for wanting to publish this book, and to my managing editor, Siobhan Drummond, for all of her help.

I thank the University of California at Davis for giving me a professional development leave of three months, which allowed this book to take shape; I also thank the H. R. Roberts Foundation for awarding me first prize in their 1992 essay contest, and Rachel Hadas for selecting me as the winner.

For friendship and help I thank Nick Birns, Allan Chinen, Emory Davis, Richard Epstein, Michael Flanagan, Chris Miller, Peter Najarian, Neil Russack, Ruth Stotter, and David Ulansey.

Special gratitude and countless debts to my dear friends: Victor Ichioka (for graphic help, among other things); Eddie Kahn, Alice Kahn, Larry Malone, and Larry Westdal; Jamie Westdal for photography; to Margaret Eldred and Eric Schroeder (who have helped me with drafts); to my sister Joan Slagle, who has lived a writing life; and especially to my sister Margaret Boe Birns, for a lifetime of inspiration. My greatest debt is to my darling daughters Lily, Amy, and Jenny, and to my beautiful wife, Judy, who is almost always my first reader, just as she has been (and is) first with me in so many ways.

Part I

Looking for the Meaning of Life

Messiness Is Next to Goddessness

MY FRIENDS DON'T BELIEVE IT, but I do occasionally clean my house. Most often, I clean when I've lost something. Cleaning up is the best way to look for something you have lost because even if you don't find the lost object, you end up with a neater house. But, even if I desperately want to find something, I stop short of a total cleanup. I follow Carl Jung's advice. He said that objects had wills of their own, so while it is all right to spend some time looking for a lost object, after a while you have to accept the fact that the lost thing wants to stay lost. For me, this means I stop cleaning up.

My second motivation for cleaning up – the impending arrival of a guest – does sometimes result in a greater effort. Of course, the amount of cleaning is directly related to how well I know the expected guest. For example, if my friend Victor is coming for dinner, I don't clean at all. But if his mother were coming over, I'd really get to work.

And in fact Victor's mother did come over to my house once. It was shortly after the birth of my first daughter, Jenny. My wife and I had stayed with Victor's mother when we had first moved to California, before we found our own apartment, and she had acted as a surrogate mother to us. So when our first child was born, we were pleased that she wanted to come see the baby. Even though Victor's mother was herself not a fanatically neat housekeeper, we wanted to present our home in a good light. For two days I put away stuff. I cleaned, I scrubbed, I vacuumed. Our house, finally presentable, welcomed Victor's mother. We were delighted to have her admire our baby.

Later we got Victor's report. When he drove his mother home, she was pleased. Nonetheless, she was slightly bothered and she wondered out loud to her son: "But I don't understand—why didn't they clean up for me?" Victor just shrugged, not having the heart to tell her the obvious truth. He'd never seen our house so clean.

I understand why he didn't dare to be totally honest with his mother. I once lied with silence in an almost identical way. Through an odd series of circumstances, I had received less than a day's notice that a camera crew from *20/20* was coming to my house to interview me. I did some serious cleaning, vacuuming, dusting, the whole bit, but most of all I hid stuff in closets. Two friends came over, bringing cardboard boxes, and we filled box after box, crammed them into closets until every closet was totally Fibber McGee'd. Then five strangers showed up, bringing TV equipment as well as a man in a suit ("Hi, I'm Bob"). The producer's assistant and I were chatting while they were setting up, and she complimented me: "You know, so many people knock themselves out cleaning up for a TV interview, but really we can shoot around anything, so it's just fine that you didn't bother." I just shrugged, as if to say, "Hey, I'm hip." I couldn't be honest. I couldn't admit that I had spent two days cleaning my house and it still looked like a mess.

A Buddhist story suggests that radical honesty about cleaning up, difficult though it may be, can bring spiritual enlightenment. The late Chogyam Trungpa, a Tibetan Buddhist lama, told a story about a spiritual hermit who lived in isolation, supported by a devotee. Usually the devotee sent a member of his family with food and other necessities for the hermit, but one day the devotee sent word that he himself would be visiting the hermit whom he had long supported. The hermit thought to himself, "Well, I'd better straighten up my room, clean my shrine." So he set to work tidying and polishing, cleaning and straightening. Soon his room, and especially the holy objects on his shrine, sparkled.

But looking around, pleased with himself, the hermit realized his room didn't look like his room anymore; everything was nice and neat, but somehow it didn't seem quite real. "What kind of a phony am I being?" he asked himself. "I'm the guru. I shouldn't be putting on this false front for anyone." So, on a mad impulse, he started messing up his room. He scattered ashes all over, especially on his shrine. He knocked things over, threw stuff around. Then the patron arrived and was genuinely impressed. "How natural you are," the patron said to the hermit, bowing. "Most people would have cleaned up for me, would have changed their natural activity to prepare for my arrival, but you, you are beyond such hypocrisy." At this the hermit burst into laughter and explained the truth to his patron: "Not only did I clean up for you, but then, reconsidering, I messed up for you as well!" They both burst into laughter and shared the experience of enlightenment.

More and more people these days have had to adjust to being messy. Not many of us any more can afford to have or be a housewife, so less and less cleaning gets done. Of course, some of the compulsively neat and fortunately rich hire maids or cleaning services. I've never seen someone who is truly messy hire a maid, though; it's only neat people who dare bring a cleaning professional into their house (frequently after having first cleaned up themselves).

I don't think neat people love things the way messy people do—why else would they constantly be putting their things away? Myself, I love things, love to have them out where I can see them, bump into them by accident, live with them. To me, a too-neat environment is sterile, and I am delighted to get home to my chaos. At age seven or so, my daughter Jenny expressed this best for me. We had returned home after a few weeks of visiting her maternal grandparents (neat people). Upon entering our apartment, she exclaimed with a sweet sigh of relief, "Ah, Messland!"

I inherited my messiness from my parents, just as my children (for better or for worse) have inherited their messiness from me. My mother liked to tell how, at a party shortly after my father had died, a woman approached her and asked, "Tell me, was your husband the man whose pants were always falling down?" I often have a similar cavalier attitude towards clothes, buttoning shirts wrong or putting them on backwards, wearing mismatched socks or generally stained clothes.

A friend of my father's once complained to him about the horrible task of cleaning out rain gutters. My father just looked bored. "Well, what do you do when your rain gutters are clogged?" the man asked my father. "I don't know that that's ever happened," my father replied (truthfully, perhaps, because we moved so frequently the rain gutters probably never had time to fill up), "but if it does happen, I guess I would have to sell the house." My father was totally serious. He would have sold his house before he'd have climbed up on a roof and cleaned out rain gutters.

It was my mother who did this sort of dirty work when it had to be done, but she was certainly not neat herself. When she was young, her mother used to give her the choice of practicing the piano or cleaning her room. She turned out to be a marvelous piano player and not a particularly fine "housekeeper." Sometimes, wearing high heels for her housework, she would clean off a table top by removing all the junk piled on it, polishing the table, then putting all the junk back on. Cleaning done.

My wife came from a neat family, but she has adapted well to life in Messland. She and I both work, of course, and we usually have other things to do than clean up. I teased my wife when I was beginning this article, saying I was including a hilarious description of how she cleaned up. Unintimidated, she responded, "I don't see how you can have any description at all of how I clean up."

Someone once defined art as the triumph over chaos. (Actually, I know who offered this definition. It was John Cheever, in a book I opened for the first time only seconds ago. For a break, I had aimlessly delved into a pile of rubble on the table next to me. Somewhere in the middle I found this paperback copy of a John Cheever book I'd bought at a garage sale. I read a page of the first story, found this definition of art, and went back to writing. Thus is the direct relation between mess and research.) But how can you triumph over chaos (make art) unless you have some chaos to begin with? For me writing has always involved an inverse relationship between the order in the room and the order on the page. Often I'll begin by straightening up a little, but as I write, the room gets messier and messier. Papers, cups, glasses, cans, old food, pencils and pens, newspapers, books seem to grow, to spread out from my desk until they fill the whole room. As the piece I'm working on gets more ordered, the room gets, with each successive draft, more disordered. When I'm finally done, clutching a few neat pages, my study looks like a bomb hit it.

Artists' studios similarly demonstrate a relationship between mess and creation. Even mathematicians' notebooks and scientists' laboratories are not as elegant and orderly as their final creations. In the tradition of the alchemists, the laboratory is still the place where the scientist "messes around" with things. And sometimes messiness is not just a byproduct of scientific invention but a necessary cause of it.

Consider, for example, Alexander Fleming's discovery of penicillin. As one of Fleming's biographers (W. Howard Hughes) put it, "Tidiness was not one of Fleming's strong points." Fleming always meant to put his used culture plates in antiseptic (preliminary to washing them) but too often would let a huge pile grow, so that those on top were completely out of the antiseptic. A colleague dropped by to visit one day, and Fleming, pointing out the pile of uncovered culture dishes, lamented: "As soon as you uncover a culture dish something tiresome is sure to happen. Things fall out of the air." (I've made the same complaint, in stronger language, about the dishes left standing too long in my sink.) Fleming, looking at his pile of messy dishes, suddenly noticed that one of them had green mold on it, around which the staphylococci colonies had disappeared. And so, because he was not tidy—because he put off doing the dishes!—Fleming discovered penicillin.

In the 1840s, Christian Schönbein, messing around (he called it experimenting) in his wife's kitchen, spilled some acid. He mopped up the mess with a handy cotton apron, then realized he should dry the apron (I guess so that his wife wouldn't discover he'd used her apron to wipe up spilled acid). When he held the wet apron over the stove, it disappeared in a smokeless explosion. Thus he had discovered how to produce nitrocellulose (guncotton), which led to the development of plastic. Goodyear's discovery of the vulcanization of rubber similarly came about because he carelessly let a mixture of soft rubber and sulfur fall on a hot stove. And according to James Watson's autobiography, when Alexander Bell inadvertently discovered that he had invented the telephone by calling out from another room, "Mr. Watson—come here—I want to see you!" he had been shouting for help because he had spilled acid on his pants.

Creativity is a messy business! Witness childbirth, the archetypal creative act (I'll leave to the reader consideration of the act that creates the child, one euphemism for which is "messing around"). Giving birth to a baby isn't all fluffy blankets and a clean cuddly little cute thing on a white sheet. It's also blood, sweat, tears, slime, afterbirth (which looks like a psychedelic eggplant), and umbilical cord. It's the archetype—to borrow Thelonius Monk's song title—of ugly beauty. It's life.

If cleanliness is next to godliness, then messiness is next to goddessness. God creates order, gives us ten neat rules carved with no crossing out in a stone tablet. The Great Goddess, on the other hand, gives us life. Henry Adams said that order produces habit, but chaos produces life. Habit (especially when connected with virtue) can be useful—do the dishes after dinner, brush your teeth, do not kill, know thy self, keep woman under rule (these last two are from Apollo's temple at Delphi); but *life* is chaotic—creative, unpredictable, uncodified.

The reality of the Goddess has been forgotten for many years, and we have all been taught to believe that neatness counts. Once upon a time, though, before humans got organized and started teaching good habits like hanging things up and putting things back, we knew about the goddess, a goddess who ruled over fertility, creativity, life, sexuality, and everything else dirty. In his book *The Origins and History of Consciousness*, Erich Neumann writes, "Whereas in the matriarchate, the pig was a favored animal sacred to the great mother goddesses Isis, Demeter, Persephone, Bona Dea, in the patriarchate it became the epitome of evil." In patriarchal religions the pig is above all unclean. And, correspondingly, God doesn't want us to live like pigs. But the pig is everywhere a symbol of fertility (pigs have lots of piglets), is associated with sexuality and the earth. Thus when Eleusis (site of the famous women's mysteries) was allowed to mint its own coins, the pig was chosen as symbol of their mysteries.

My wife and I love it when, for brief moments, our house is relatively neat. One doesn't always want to live like a pig. But the compulsion to always have a neat house is like the compulsion to be thin. Neatness is fine, and so is thinness—but food is so good, life is so full. The Goddess wants us to create, to enjoy the fruits of the earth, not to make perfect order, but to make full and whole lives.

Reference

Neumann, Erich. *The Origins and History of Consciousness.* London: Routledge & Kegan Paul, 1954, 1982.

Mistakes Were Made: Philosophy in an Off Key

WHENEVER ANYONE USED THE word *funny* when I was little, my sisters and I would of course immediately ask, "Funny ha ha or funny peculiar?" This distinction seems a bit artificial to me now: I think that to be funny ha ha you must also be a bit funny peculiar, a bit off (maybe that's why, when I'm leaving somewhere, I say, "I'm off"). I'm a person who has always been funny (in both senses). As a child, like any child, I first made people laugh inadvertently, by making mistakes (growing alarmed, for example, after hearing some radio voice speculate about the possibility of red gorillas invading us). Then I realized that I could be intentionally funny just by listening to the mistakes made in my mind, picking out the ones that struck me funny, then saying them out loud. I learned to be funny by paying attention to my mistakes.

Dave Brubeck once said that he thought improvisation came originally from the musician hearing his or her own mistakes, then consciously repeating them, seeking out the nicer ones. Most of us don't like to admit our mistakes, so we teach ourselves not to notice them. But we all make mistakes every day, and in many ways these mistakes are our creativity, our improvisations off the standard theme, our uniqueness. Everyone is "funny." (Freud, of course, suggested this, arguing that we are all by definition neurotic—unless we are psychotic—and that consciousness itself is a mistake leading inevitably to discontent.) We all do and think funny things every day, only most of us edit them out of our consciousness, don't share some of the most interesting things we think and do.

For example, in 1981 I heard that my wife was expecting our third child, and I was suddenly filled with the archetypal need to make money. The English department of the University of California at Davis had advertised for "visiting lecturers" to teach composition. They were not interviewing, their job announcement said, but would be happy to talk if you happened to be in the area. I drove an hour from my Berkeley home so as to happen to be in the area, parked by the pathogen-free pig barn, then wandered across campus until I found Sproul Hall, home of the English department. The chair, Professor Hanzo, was surprised to have someone drop in, but he was gracious. After an amiable chat, he took me in to meet the director of composition, with whom I discussed curriculum. I was hired.

When the quarter started, I tried to look the part of a college teacher (the seventies were over). I got a haircut, wore a sports jacket, carried a briefcase (bought at a garage sale). I brought a bag lunch each day (which, I confess, my wife packed for me). She also packed me an orange folding umbrella so that in the event of a sudden rain, I wouldn't be soaked. About six weeks into the quarter came the day of the English department potluck, which I thought I was supposed to attend in order to meet my colleagues. I was walking across the quad to my last class of the day when out of the skies came torrential rain, a serious downpour. I stopped to reach down into my briefcase for my orange folding umbrella. I quickly took it out, then struggled to get it open. I have never been very good with mechanical things, so I was not surprised when I couldn't immediately open it. I was, however, surprised to find myself imagining that my orange folding umbrella was actually a carrot. I dismissed this as a fantasy, a hallucination or a flashback, and refocused my eyes on my umbrella. But as I struggled to open that orange folding umbrella—where was the damn button?—it kept trying to turn back into a carrot. For a brief while (maybe ten seconds) I was able to continue convincing myself that it *was* an umbrella, but finally I had to admit to myself that I was indeed standing in the middle of the quad in the middle of a rainstorm trying to unfurl a carrot over my head. Later I decided that if I had had tenure I would have boldly lifted that carrot above my head and walked, dry in my own mind, to class. As it was, I put my carrot away, looked around sheepishly to see if anyone was staring at me, and hurried on in the rain.

I spent the first part of the class—I think it was advanced composition—talking about my experience, talking about mistakes and the power of the imagination. I had been deluded, no doubt, but I was amazed to see that my mind could, if only for brief moments, transform reality. How wonderful was fantasy! I wondered how often we have such mini-hallucinations, such misperceptions, and ignore them, refusing to submit to the mind's transforming capacity. I also wondered how often we see what we want to see—I had so wanted to see an umbrella!—rather than what's really there. My class was no doubt befuddled, but they were amused and interested. They participated happily in the discussion, and I eventually steered the hour back to what was on the syllabus.

After class, it was raining even harder. I held my briefcase over my head, walking through newly created lakes in the middle of the quad, completely soaking my pants. I went up to my office and closed the door. I was bedraggled, soaking wet, and I had to wait two more hours for the potluck. The potluck! I didn't want to show up soaking wet. That would not impress my colleagues. I looked around my office and saw the heater under the window. I would dry my pants! I checked to make sure my door was locked, took off my pants, and hung them from the curtain rod. I turned the heater up full blast and sat at my desk, pleased, grading papers in my underwear. Suddenly I looked up and realized I should pull the curtains so people on the quad didn't wonder about the trousers hanging in the window. Then I went back to my papers.

After some minutes came a knock on my door. I wasn't holding office hours. No one knew I was here. But the knocking persisted. Like the porter in *Macbeth*, I could not remain silent. "Who's there?"

A young man gave his name, but I didn't recognize it.

"I'm in your advanced composition class."

"Really? I don't remember you. Anyway, I'm not holding office hours now, so you'll have to see me on Monday."

"Mr. Boe! I need to talk to you now! I know I've missed a bunch of your classes. I was sick, then I got behind, but I can make up the work. I need this course to graduate, and this is my last quarter here. Today's the last day to drop classes so if you won't let me make up the work, I have to drop today, before five o'clock. And it's almost 4:30 now! Couldn't I talk with you for just five minutes?"

"Just a second," I said and got up to get my pants. My pants, however, had dried into a tight knot on the curtain rod. I struggled to get them untied.

As I struggled, the knocking resumed.

"Just a minute!" I shouted. But I couldn't get my trousers untied from the curtain rod.

"Mr. Boe. Please. I have to talk with you now. The office closes at 5, so if I'm going to drop . . ."

I gave up, walked to the door, and opened it a crack. I explained, as best I could, my situation. "If you don't mind me holding office hours in my underwear," I said, "I'd be happy to talk with you."

He didn't seem particularly bothered. Indeed he hardly seemed to notice. We sat down and he explained his situation. Amazingly, he and I quickly came to agree that his writing was important, that he couldn't learn what he needed to learn if he had to catch up with four missed weeks of work. He would drop the course, staying in school to take it again the next quarter—he hoped with me. He shook my hand as he left, but I didn't get up.

I eventually did get my pants untied and went to the potluck. Few of my colleagues were there, and I doubt if they would have noticed me if I had come soaking wet or even in my underwear.

Often in the ten subsequent years I've taught at U. C. Davis, I've had to counsel students who want to make up a lot of work in a brief period of time, who don't want to have to take a course over. The student always wants to make up the work, write three papers in an evening, and get the requirement out of the way. I usually think the student should drop the course and do it right in a subsequent quarter. I especially think this if the student's writing is problematical, as this young man's was. I knew he *needed* the course. But he knew he wanted to graduate *that* quarter. I've never since had such ease in persuading a student to do the pedagogically right but practically difficult thing. I can only conclude that the secret of my success was in the series of mistakes which led me to hold an office hour in my underwear and in the openness and honesty this situation engendered.

While by definition mistakes are to be regretted, one of the ironic pleasures of aging is to look back fondly on the mistakes of youth. I find it odd that many young people today seem to be trying to avoid mistakes, working assiduously to avoid wasting their youth. This is no doubt a mistake on their parts. As one of the hippie generation, I have, of course, a wasted past to look back on. Indeed one favorite metaphor for the euphoric state we sought was "wasted." To get really wasted seemed, for some odd reason, the appropriate thing to do.

I remember one such wasted day in the early seventies, when the spirit of the sixties had flowered but not yet wilted. Inspired by Carlos Castaneda, I had eaten several peyote buds. I was on the porch of my apartment, holding my less-than-one-year-old, Amy. For some reason I desperately wanted her to see a bird. I kept pointing them out to her, but she seemed not to notice them, so small, so far away. I turned to go in, and as I got to the door, two birds suddenly swooped onto the porch, wings flapping, apparently fighting. We turned around, staring at a blur of birds. Immediately I called to my wife and my other daughter Jenny. They came running and, of course, as they ran onto the porch, the birds flew away. Only then did I realize one or both of these birds must have been Mescalito. Mescalito always appears when you eat peyote, Castaneda taught, but I, an amateur, had not been ready. Instead of speaking to the birds, asking for their teaching, I mistakenly (bourgeois!) had called to my family.

Much later, that night, I lay in bed, tired but wired, while my wife and kids slept. Unable to sleep myself, I started to reread Castaneda's *A Separate Reality*. I was reading very slowly, alternately thinking and spacing out. Ah, the brave new worlds open to the daring. Suddenly, in the midst of my reverie, I noticed on the wall behind me just above my shoulder a large cockroach. In a flash, fueled by innate fear and hatred of insects, I slapped the book against the wall, squashing the cockroach into a vile, black mush.

After disposing of the body and settling down with my book again, I began to regret. Doesn't Castaneda teach us to be open to Mescalito in whatever form he might appear? Didn't the Guardian (in the very chapter I had been reading) appear to Carlos as a gnat? And I realized this was the very first cockroach I had ever seen in my apartment. It had obviously been a messenger. I should have at least tested it, spoken to it, asked for a lesson. But instead, I acted like a fascist, with bigoted hatred of insects. . . After some minutes of self-recrimination, I went back to the book.

In a little while, there suddenly appeared on the wall above my shoulder another large cockroach. Without a moment's hesitation, I slammed the book against the wall, squashing this second insect to death. Again I was filled with remorse. Had I squashed a guardian, or Mescalito himself? But now at least I knew that there was no hope of me changing, no point in any more spiritual cockroaches appearing to me again. Given the chance, I would make this same mistake eternally, would like some dilettante spiritual Sisyphus, forever and ever squash any insect messengers.

Regret is my favorite contemplative mode. I love the fantasy that I learn from my mistakes—that even if I don't always learn not to repeat the same mistake over and over, I learn through regret who I am. Our mistakes are what we are, are what define our personalities. After a time, I accepted my squashing of Mescalito as part of the definition of who I was—married, a father of two, more an intellectual worrier than a spiritual warrior. And really, given my city life, it was more important to kill the first cockroach invaders to my apartment than to try to communicate with the other reality. So I learned, despite my spiritual inclinations, to accept and even be grateful for some of my obvious limitations.

Once, while visiting my family in New Jersey, I had a dream in which the Angel of Life appeared to me and revealed the three secrets of the universe. Really. The Angel of Life clad in luminescent white told me the three secrets of the universe! The dream stunned me awake. I meditated on the meaning of the three secrets, feeling their depth and profundity sear into my very being. I tossed and turned, wondering why I had been selected to be told. Finally, after what seemed like hours of thought, I was able to fall back asleep.

When I awoke in the morning, I had forgotten two of the angel's secrets. Of course, I regretted my foolishness in not writing down the three secrets (I had thought I could never forget them), but I eventually came to accept this mistake as, once more, an indication of who I am. Since the first secret was almost more than I could handle, it was probably for the best that I forgot two-thirds of the angel's message.

The secret I remembered, as revealed by the angel, was, "When the earth shatters, the atmosphere survives." The indecipherability only partially consoled me for my failure to remember the other two secrets (I was sure, of course, that they had made perfect sense). A few days after the dream, however, I made a mistake that revealed to me the meaning of the angel's words and almost cost me my life.

I was spending the day at the seashore with my family. The ocean was very rough that day, and no one had been able (or wanted) to swim beyond the point where the waves were breaking.

I'm a fairly strong swimmer so, leaving my brother behind, I battled the waves out into the deep. For a few minutes, I floated free and alone. Then as the waves started breaking directly over me, I realized I had made a mistake in swimming out so far. I tried to swim in, but a strong undertow kept pulling me back out. Soon I was swallowing salt water, gasping for air, and getting very tired. Bobbing up between waves, I saw my brother on the shore and waved wildly, screaming above the surf, as loud as I could, "HEEELLLLP!" Our eyes met over the distance. I saw him lift his arm and wave hello. Here I was dying, and he thought I was just showing off.

Now I was in full panic, fighting, screaming, gagging, choking. But all my striving was useless. I moved no closer to the shore, and I knew I was drowning, that there was no hope. The waves seemed huge. A giant one washed over me, and I screamed once more for help, but my body was no longer really fighting. As the wave washed over me, I heard a voice inside me, a part of my own self, say very clearly, very calmly, "Oh, he's drowning now. I guess I'll be going." I was literally screaming in panic even as this voice within me was detached, calm, uncaring. Then another huge wave washed over and, having ceased struggling, I floated upon and within it toward the shore. I staggered to my feet, waded into shore, trying to seem dignified, embarrassed to admit what everyone could see immediately—that I had almost drowned.

Later that night, I thought about this experience in terms of the angel's message: "When the earth shatters, the atmosphere survives." As I was drowning, a part of me certainly thought that it was going to survive. Thus "when the earth shatters" would mean "when the body dies," and "the atmosphere survives" would mean "the spirit/soul lives on." Because I had made the mistake of swimming out too far in a rough sea, I was able, perhaps, to decipher one of the secrets of the universe. But I could find very little consolation, somehow, in this voice that expected to survive after I had drowned. Here I was, about to die, and it calmly says, "Well, so long." I truly believed that if my immortal soul were about to perish, I'd be a little less detached, a little less like a rat leaving a sinking ship.

I was not on good terms with the spirit/soul part of me for some time after that. I'd tell myself that I only survived because my "soul" left me and I quit struggling (and so was washed to safety), but really I think it was the other way around: once I quit struggling and was ready to die, my soul decided it was time to cut out. I knew one was supposed to think kindly about one's immortal soul, but it surely hadn't seemed very concerned about me.

As a young man there had been other times (like the time I slipped on a waterfall) I came close to dying, but this experience sort of woke me up. When the earth shatters, the atmosphere may survive, but I was still awfully fond of the earth, of life. One spiritual secret was more than enough for me. I was going to worry about number one for awhile and let my soul (number two) take care of itself.

A few months ago I had a dream which is, in fact, the genesis of this essay. I was in line with a bunch of other people to ask Carl Jung a question. Unfortunately, I never got my turn, but the woman directly in front of me did. She asked Jung, "When do you achieve your self?" Jung answered, "When you're old and wrinkly, and your face and eyes get all twinkly, and you look at everything as if it were a mistake."

To achieve your true self is to realize that everything is a mistake. Every day is a mistake, civilization is a mistake, nature is a beautiful mistake. To do something is a mistake, not to do anything is certainly a mistake. I remember hearing how the Navaho would always weave a mistake into their rugs. The commentators I read said this was so that they wouldn't be showing hubris, competing with the gods, but I think it was just a sign of their artfulness, their realism. There's always a mistake in everything; to make a perfect rug is just not the way things are. For me, part of Shakespeare's power is in what seem to be his mistakes, the parts of his plays that to scholars (and no doubt to his contemporaries) still don't quite make sense. Shakespeare didn't seem to bother with getting it perfect, with always getting the plot consistent and the language coherent. To eliminate mistakes is to eliminate life.

Gertrude Stein wrote:

> The care with which the rain is wrong, and the green is wrong and the white is wrong, the care with which there is a chair and plenty of breathing. The care with which there is incredible justice and likeness, all this makes a magnificent asparagus, and also a fountain.

It's all wrong, everything, beautifully and carefully wrong, and all these individual wrongnesses make up our incredible world of asparagus, fountains, dreams, justice, Gertrude Stein, music, etc.

Music is a good metaphor for our mistaken world. The beauty of music is not dependent on precisely following the perfect laws of acoustical physics. After all, most of the world's pianos are necessarily slightly out of tune, slightly off. You see, pianos are tempered: the intervals (half-tones) are set precisely the same so that the instrument can play equally well in a variety of keys. This makes the piano's fifths and thirds all a little off from the perfect fifths and thirds of physics. But by tuning our pianos (and many other modern Western instruments) so that they are a little off, by adopting a necessarily imperfect tuning system, we allow for greater communication. We allow various instruments to play together in various keys, to make beautiful music that is always a little off.

As Wordsworth complained in a beautifully musical sonnet, "for everything, we are out of tune." Even our own earth's orbit around the sun is a little off, not a perfect circle. Nor are the earth, the sun, and the moon perfect spheres. The earth in its lovely spin wobbles just a bit. Everything's off, and so am I.

References

Stein, Gertrude. *Tender Buttons: Objects, Food, Rooms.* New York: Random House, Vintage Editions, 1972.

Wordsworth, William. "The world is too much with us: late and soon." In *The Prelude with a Selection from the Shorter Poems*, Carlos Baker, ed. New York: Holt, Rinehart and Winston, 1966.

For Me and My Anima

I WOKE UP IN THE MIDDLE OF THE night. I took a drink of water from the glass on my nightstand. Then, rolling over to go back to sleep, I glanced at the woman in bed next to me. I blinked my eyes hard and looked again. I had never seen this woman before in my life! I stared at her. What was this strange woman doing in bed next to me? I didn't know, but suddenly I didn't care. She was asleep. She was in my bed. What the hell—I decided to kiss her. I leaned across her sleeping body, boldly pressing my lips against hers. Within moments, to my surprise and delight, she started kissing me back. After the kiss, she smiled up at me and opened her eyes. To my shock, I saw that I had been kissing my wife.

Of course I won't say I was disappointed, but I certainly felt a diminished nervous excitement and less sense of daring. I wondered who the strange woman was and what had become of her. But as things turned out, I had little time right then to ponder such problems.

No doubt I had been in one of those states between sleeping and waking where, even though my eyes were open, I was still more or less dreaming. The strange woman I thought I was kissing would then have been an image in my own unconscious. Jung has said that we all have such a person in us (we are socialized to identify our selves with one sex, and the other sex becomes personified in the unconscious as our anima or animus). So the strange woman I had been kissing was what Jung would call my anima. It can be a shock for a man to discover he is kissing an actual woman and not his inner image of a woman. I think the practical lesson, for men and for women, is that you are not always kissing the one you think you are kissing.

A while ago I was talking to a co-worker and good friend of mine in the hall outside her office. As we were chatting, she suddenly put her hand down the front of her blouse. I was disconcerted and, of course, interested, but I tried to continue the conversation. As we talked, she continued reaching down in her blouse, exploring around her breasts. Was this some sort of office foreplay, a prelude to more exciting events? (Why hadn't I read that book on body language!) Amazingly, we continued talking during her self-exploration. I was consciously paying attention to our rational conversation, but my eyes were riveted on her hand down her blouse, my deeper self delving between her breasts. Then suddenly she gave a little gasp (I was ready to gasp, too) and pulled out a spider, which she quickly threw on the floor.

Being the gentleman I am, I rushed to tell this story to everyone else in the office. She turned a bit red but laughed good-naturedly, saying that she was glad I'd "got my jollies" out of the scene, but she was certainly not going to stand still when there was a spider between her breasts.

Really though, "jollies" doesn't do justice to the fascination she evoked, to how deeply she engaged my attention. Even though I was still actively engaged in our conversation, my unconscious was suddenly activated. As Freud repeatedly showed, our unconscious mind is deeply stirred by sexuality. But I wasn't merely being "turned on" or getting my "jollies" as one might in instinctively responding to blatant sexuality. I was fascinated in part because I was mystified. The anima personifies the combination of mystery and sexuality man finds in woman. For a few moments, as she reached inside her blouse, she was no longer my friend and co-worker. I was in the presence of an archetype: anima.

Ever year my family and three other families go for a weekend camping trip. We hike a little way into the backcountry, but the men make numerous trips back to the car for ice, beer, gin, brandy, and other necessities (stuffed animals, extra diapers, food). At night we sit around the fire, drinking tea or brandy and talking, while various of us cuddle children or go off to tuck them into sleeping bags.

On one such night, my wife left to put our toddler Lily to sleep. When she returned I was still drinking my brandy, trading stories around the fire. Naturally enough, as I talked I stroked her leg up around the thigh. This was really more an affectionate than an amorous gesture, an almost unconscious husbandly act.

After fifteen minutes or so, with the fire starting to die down, I looked over at my wife to suggest maybe we should go to bed, too. But it was not my wife sitting next to me! She was still putting Lily to sleep (probably had fallen asleep herself), and one of my friends' wives (actually the woman I knew least well in the group) had sat down next to me.

I immediately withdrew my hand from her leg. But then I was presented with a dilemma. I'm not the kind of man who casually puts his hand on women's legs (much as I would like to), so I felt that I should explain my unusual behavior. But I couldn't apologize without insulting her. I certainly couldn't say, "I'd never have had my hand on your leg if I had know it was you," or even, "I was only fondling your thigh because I thought you were my wife." So I looked the other way, said nothing and had another glass of brandy.

The irony was that if I had know it was a strange woman and not my wife, I'd have certainly been paying more attention to my fondling. Come to think of it, I would have been fascinated (probably because the "strange woman" more easily carries the image of the anima). As it was, she must have been surprised at my casual, even offhand, touching of her leg. I hope she was at least paying more attention than I was (maybe I should have asked her if I seemed to be enjoying myself).

Mistaken identity is a time-honored love theme (see, for example, Genesis with Leah's substitution for Rachel as Jacob's bride, or Shakespeare's *All's Well That Ends Well*). Maybe this theme has something to do with the anima, with teaching us that the object of our affection is not always who we consciously think it is. To put it in psychological terms, our sexual feelings are dependent on inner images that we unconsciously project onto outer reality.

I remember a friend of mine telling how he was sitting next to a beautiful woman on a long bus ride. They struck up a conversation, one thing led to another, and soon they were making out. He was having a great time, feeling he had truly gotten lucky. The bus made a rest stop, and the woman left to go to the ladies room. An older fellow approached my friend, saying, "You know that's a man, don't you?"

Suddenly my friend didn't feel so lucky. It was the same person coming out of the ladies room, but now, given his sexual orientation, my friend changed seats. You've probably heard variations on this story (that compendium of folklore known as the *National Enquirer* loves those versions where the groom only discovers the true sex of his bride on the wedding night). These stories capture the attitude of heterosexual men. Like my friend on the bus, I guess I too would only kiss a man if he were successfully disguised in women's clothes. Then I would have a more suitable hook for my inner image of the feminine.

I often talk in my sleep. I rarely remember what I've said, but my wife fills me in. I figure these sleeptalkings are, like dreams, messages from the unconscious.

One morning my wife reported that in the middle of the night I woke her and asked her if she was a girl. When she sleepily said yes, I kissed her so hard I left a bruise on her lip. (She did have such a bruise in the morning, and I accept her word that I had caused it.)

I find it interesting that even in a deep sleep I first checked for the proper sex. Actually I *only* checked for the proper sex. I do have a personal relationship with my wife, thank you, but the evidence suggests I also have a primal longing for woman (or maybe it's It—or id, or the unconscious—that longs for woman).

Another morning my wife told me that in the middle of the night I had awakened her and asked her who she was. She gave her name, but I seemed not really to recognize it. "Hey, whoever you are, come here," I finally said, putting my arm around her. And, she admitted to me in the morning, she was happy to be cuddled, even in this seemingly impersonal way.

The inner image of woman (the anima) can be projected on any female (women have complained about this for years, although not using Jung's terminology). I *can* be discriminating and personal in my relationships with specific women. Still, there is often something collective or primal in the male-female relationship (I guess this is most obvious in the sex act itself). Even as I relate to specific women, my unconscious is relating to woman. And this woman is an inner image, my anima. It's the same old story: I love my wife, but oh you anima.

Religion and Basketball

ON ANY GIVEN SABBATH DAY people gather to watch ball games. In many ways these games are pagan substitutes for the collective religious experience of church. I've often seen newspaper photos of basketball games—the eyes of all the players and all the fans are fixed upon the ball frozen above the rim. When the game is on TV there are millions of eyes focused upon that same ball. This is a *collective* spiritual experience; the group consciousness is united by a single thing, the ball. The ball acts like the *mandala* in Tibetan systems of concentration and meditation, focusing the psyche of the individual, uniting the consciousness of the group.

Shortly before his death, Black Elk, a priest of the Oglala Sioux, gave an account of the seven rites of his people. These were recorded and edited by Joseph Brown in *The Sacred Pipe*. The seventh and last rite is a game that was revealed in a vision, "The Throwing of the Ball." A ball is painted red (the color of the world), and in blue (the color of the heavens) there are made dots at the four quarters. Then by making two blue circles going all around the ball, Heaven and Earth are united into one sacred ball. (This ball makes me wish our culture had a symbolic ball, perhaps a whole earth ball, a rubber, bouncing globe.) In the Sioux rite, a little girl takes the ball, which is both the world and the great spirit, *Wakan-Tanka*, and throws it to the west, where whoever is lucky enough to catch it embraces it and offers it to the six directions (east, west, north, south, up, and down) and gives it back to the girl. She then throws it to the north and to the other directions. Black Elk explains this rite: "Just as the ball is thrown from the center to the quarters, so *Wakan-Tanka* is at every direction and is everywhere in the world; and as the ball descends upon the people so does His power, which is only received by a very few people, especially in these last days."

In the vision which gave birth to this game, the little girl who threw the ball turned into a buffalo calf, nudged the ball towards the man, and said: "This universe really belongs to the two-leggeds, for we four-legged people cannot play with a ball." Black Elk says that this is true because of all creatures in the universe, "it is the two-legged men alone who, if they purify and humiliate themselves, may become one with — or may know — *Wakan-Tanka*." The unique spiritual capacity of us two-legged ones is symbolically related to our ability to play ball; we are the creature who plays with a ball (the symbolic union of heaven and earth), and so the universe belongs to us. *The Sacred Pipe* ends with Black Elk's moving words: "At this sad time today among our own people, we are scrambling for the ball, and some are not even trying to catch it, which makes me cry when I think of it. But soon I know it will be caught, for the end is rapidly approaching, and then it will be returned to the center, and our people will be with it. It is my prayer that this be so, and it is in order to aid in this recovery of the ball, that I have wished to make this book."

I sometimes feel, when I play basketball, that I am in some large sense trying to recover the ball. To play well is to unite body and mind; to play badly is to be out of Tao. What a fine feeling it is to go up for a jump shot and as you release the ball to know it is going in, to be able to say in your mind or out loud, "Swish." Sometimes you don't even need to see the basket; you can go up for a shot with a defender or the sun in your eyes and still know the ball is going in. It almost feels as if there is telekinesis involved; you think the ball into the basket. I play basketball in order to experience those moments when I feel in rhythm, and it is more a matter of the rhythm having me than of my having the rhythm. I find myself moving to the open spot at the right time and putting the ball surely in the empty circle that the rim defines. The experience is like that described in *Zen and the Art of Archery*: It moves me on the court, It shoots the ball.

Usually you don't have time to think out what you are going to do; you move and react instinctively, unconsciously. At magic moments, you and your teammates can seem to read each other's minds; you can throw a blind pass knowing that a teammate will have moved to that spot. You feel a part of a greater whole, a group mind, a Team. But while It may shoot the ball, and It may move you on the court, consciousness is not eliminated. What is demanded is a sort of union of consciousness and unconsciousness; you can perceive and analyze, discuss and plan, but the analyses and plans have to blend with unconscious knowledge in a flow and rhythm. In the flow of a five-man team, you sink to the level of group mind while at the same time intensifying your own individual concentration, heightening your own consciousness by focusing it on the narrow field of a basketball game

People often talk about rhythm and flow in basketball. And when playing basketball you do indeed feel the rhythm, flow with the group mind in a way that is much like improvising music in a small group; you are all improvising together, paying attention to each other and to the structure of the game (or the music), trying to let the It within the individual you direct your flow, all the while maintaining awareness of what the group is actual doing. And the problem in both music and basketball often is playing *together*. It can be relatively easy (in music or basketball) to "synch" in to someone with whom you have played a lot before. If you two can play together as a unit, then that dual unity can reach out to include a third, and eventually, hopefully, the whole team will be playing together.

The ball is the focus of the group consciousness; it is *Wakan-Tanka*, the great mandala. A basic rule of defense is to see the ball; even when watching your own man, you must be conscious of the ball. On offense, to have the ball is to be the center of attention. It is easy to understand how difficult it can be for gifted offensive players to learn the selfless art of giving up the ball.

My favorite way of passing is to jump into the air, hang in mid-air as if preparing to shoot, and as the defense freezes awaiting the shot, pass off. The sensation of hanging in the air before shooting or passing is one of the most pleasurable in basketball. When you are hanging in the air, time can seem to stretch out as the moment fills with the perception of alternatives. Oscar Robertson, a truly great if not flashy ballplayer, urged players never to go up into the air unless they knew what they were going to do with the ball. More and more contemporary players choose the pleasure and uncertainty of going up in the air in order to create a situation, deciding what to do when in full flight. As a player, I have an ambivalent attitude towards flying; it is such a pleasure that I sometimes leave my feet too often, get hung up in the air with nothing to do with the ball. The problem of when to fly and when to stay grounded is a symbolic one for me: I have had to learn, in my nonathletic life as well, when to keep my feet on the ground.

Julius Erving, "Dr. J," says, "My game is in the air." Dr. J was probably the first player to fly obviously, to really defy the laws of gravity. Scientists used to say a baseball couldn't curve, just as they still say a person can't fly; but certain basketball players do sometimes fly, or so it seems. Dr. J inspired me to write a little poem in which I envisioned a great basketball player of the far future: "Wondrous birdman, enlightened athlete-monk, / Flying through the air and then, slam-dunk!" I love the vision of some future shaman-athlete. Flying has always been a symbol of spiritual power: in many cultures the shaman was the birdman, the man who could fly. I only wish that the symbolic flying power of current players was matched by flights of consciousness, of spiritual soaring.

Like many men, I root for my team as an adult just as I rooted for my team a child, with an almost religious fervor. Since I live in the San Francisco Bay Area, I root for the Golden State Warriors. The Warriors are not so much my team as my totem. Sports teams, so often named after animals, are totems of our specific areas, magical representatives of a certain group of people. I know my friends and I felt uplifted, blessed with luck (the gift of the gods) when, in 1975, the Warriors won the championship. I hope that blessing returns some day.

To go to a ball game is to participate in a primitive rite, a Dionysian revel. The Oakland Coliseum where my totem team plays takes on a ceremonial character. Between the parking lot and the arena there is a long winding row of small, stone, penis-shaped pillars. In India, they would be recognized immediately as what they are, *lingams*, ceremonial stone phalluses. Ascending along the line of lingams, you approach the great round colossus, the Coliseum, looking like the Great Mother at the end of a row of her sons.

After giving your ticket to the gatekeeper, you pass into the other, ceremonial realm. The attendants help the confused find their way through the maze of seats and sections to their spot. Down below, at the bottom of the great circle that is the Coliseum, there is the rectangular court. As a magic space with its own center circle, the rectangular court within the circular building suggests the proverbial squared circle. At a prearranged time, the players symmetrically distribute themselves around the middle of the symmetrical court. The referee throws the ball about the exact center of the court and the game begins. Anyone profane enough to step onto the sacred space during the game will, of course, be subject to ejection and arrest. The players move in waves, from north to south and south to north, as all attention focuses upon the special space, with its special rules and its own time frame. As the game progresses the crowd becomes less inhibited; an exciting playoff game can almost *possess* a crowd. Conscious control slips away, mass mind takes over. There can be a wonderful relief or purge involved in this sinking into unconsciousness, as a mass of people focus on a simple game; it can also be rather frightening, as primitive emotions surge to the surface.

This game, basketball, was invented by James Naismith in 1891, in Springfield, Massachusetts. While Dr. Naismith deserves credit for his invention and ingenuity, in some ways the roots of basketball reach into Native American culture. It is important to realize that before the discovery of the "New World" there was no rubber in Europe. Rubber was called "India rubber" because it was first brought to Europe from the West Indies, the land Columbus mistakenly thought was India. Archaeological evidence suggests that rubber was used by the Maya perhaps as early as the 11th century. The rubber ball is a Native American invention, and a hoop game with a rubber ball was popular throughout Native American culture.

The Native Americans played a number of different rubber ball games, but I am interested in one which used a stone ring through which the rubber ball was to be propelled. There was no real parallel to the use of a ring in European games, so early observers tended to focus on this aspect also. The game, which was played throughout Mexico, was like a combination of basketball and volleyball. The object was to score points by sending the ball into the opposing team's court so that it could not be returned. Generally the ball was struck with the hips, buttocks, or knee; to use the hands or other part of the body was to forfeit a point. There was a stone ring in each team's court, and if a player sent the ball through the ring (a very difficult feat), he won the game outright. Such a lucky player had the right to claim gifts from the losing team (who would abuse him as bewitched and run away), and he would be honored by his teammates. He would also make sacrifices to the game's patron deity and to the stone ring itself.

The magical-religious elements in the ancient rubber ball games are obvious. Every court had images of the patron deity (or deities) of the game. Players might magically prepare the game balls the night before a game and ask for supernatural help during the game. The referees were likely to be priests.

But if the magical-religious element in the ancient games is obvious, so is the aggressive component. The players understood the game to symbolize warfare, and sometimes it would even be used as a substitute for warfare. The duality implicit in this and similar competitive games was rendered conscious by making the god of twins a deity of the game. The game itself was quite violent in that the ball (often made of solid rubber) was heavy enough to cause serious injury (and even death) to a player struck in the wrong place. And like the rubber ball games played in America today, the Native American rubber ball games were inextricably linked to gambling. Players and spectators inevitably wagered upon the outcome and therefore used all their aggressive energy and magical power to achieve victory.

Like the ancient American rubber ball games, the modern American rubber ball game of basketball involves competitive as well as religious energy, combines aggression and ritual. I love the intensity with which I play and watch basketball, but I must admit that my attempts to see basketball as a religion are inadequate. Basketball is a very *primitive* spiritual event. Anthropologists have traditionally seen the Native American rubber ball games as *primitive* religious and secular events, but those players were at least conscious of the spiritual symbolism of their game and court. I write here in an attempt to make conscious some of the spiritual implications in my game, basketball. Basketball does play an important part in my spiritual life; but I am sometimes saddened to admit how limited, primitive, and unconscious that spiritual life really is. The problem comes, I think, from the way in which the spiritual has been cut off from the secular. In our modern world it is unnaturally difficult to see the spiritual dimension in anything so secular as a ball game (or a dance, a carnival, a party). In Europe as late as the 16th century, there were ceremonial ball-dances held in churches. Priests danced to the rhythm of the chant, and a ball was thrown or handed around. This game was finally banned as secular, not "spiritual" enough for priests and churches. We have forgotten that the Olympics are in honor of the Great God; we have separated the secular from the spiritual. I envy those so-called "primitive" cultures where this division was not so clear cut. I can only wish, with Black Elk, that we might begin to try to recover the ball.

References

Black Elk. 1971. *The Sacred Pipe: Black Elk's Account of the Seven Rites of the Oglala Sioux*. Recorded and edited by Joseph Epes Brown. New York: Penguin Books.

Herrigel, Eugen. 1958. *Zen and the Art of Archery*. New York: Pantheon Books.

Stern, Theodore. 1966. *The Rubber-Ball Games of the Americas*. Seattle: University of Washington Press.

The Holidays of Darkness

I WAS DRIVING WITH MY FRIEND Eddie back from George's Orange in Dixon, the best Mexican restaurant I've ever been to. We were full of chiles rellenos, chimichangas, and beer. It was getting late, and we slid into the easiest conversation: moaning over the prospect of Christmas. Eddie more than anyone I know finds spending money morally reprehensible. So, of course, he hates buying gifts and even getting them (he's willing to accept consumables, for then he knows the gift will soon disappear). But Eddie admitted to me, as we drove toward home, that even he was willing to go through the pain of Christmas, for he knew it was necessary to buy off the forces of darkness.

All of the dying year's holidays are really about buying off (or propitiating) the forces of darkness. First there's Halloween. On Halloween my wife usually takes our littlest one out trick-or-treating, and I stay home with my dog Boz. For Boz, a procession of costumed strangers appearing at our door involves real terror. And I imagine that Boz helps the children get a little genuine terror, too, for as they reach for the candy, they always keep one eye on the snarling little dog I am constantly kicking back from them. My home being in Berkeley, there is always sometime during the evening a costumed adult accompanying some costumed children. This year it was a grown man dressed in a devil suit. I gave the children their candy (little Snickers bars), but the man refused to take any. At this madness on his part, I grew emotional: "Don't you understand?" I screamed. "This is part of a ritual. If you come to my door dressed as an evil spirit, you must let me propitiate you. Take a piece of candy." I don't think he knew what *propitiate* meant, but looking surprisingly frightened for a devil, he took the candy and left.

Halloween stems from the old Celtic new year's eve, Samhain. October 31st, November night, was the night the fairies left their summer abode to move indoors, usually inside the hills (on May Day, summer began, and the fairies left their winter abode). This division of the year into two seasons certainly fits my San Francisco Bay Area consciousness, where winter can begin and summer can end around the beginning of November.

October 31st, new year's eve, is thus the night the fairies are about. Fairies, of course, are "the good people." But we call them the good people much as the ancient Greeks called the furies (horrible agents of divine vengeance) "the kindly ones." You don't want to get the fairies mad at you—they can be rather dangerous—so it's best to call them, euphemistically, the good people.

On Halloween, we have a ritual. The little ones (hopefully the most innocent of us) dress up as the dangerous dark spirits. These evil spirits come to our house, and if we give them a gift, a sweet, then maybe they won't trick us. This is the magic ritual to deal with the evil in the air on October 31st, the eve of dark November.

Halloween is traditionally the last outdoor holiday; just as the fairies changed their abode, so too were the animals brought inside to barns or slaughtered for a harvest festival. Astrologically, this harvest time belongs to Scorpio. Scorpio is ruled by Pluto, god of the underworld. Pluto is traditionally confused with Plutus, the god of wealth, and this confusion is not unreasonable. The goods of the earth, the stuff in the cornucopia, have their roots underground, and the fertility of life is based on death.

The uniquely American harvest festival, Thanksgiving, is, like all the winter holidays, another vestigial new year's eve. Darkness and cold grow, and we kill a million turkeys and gorge ourselves in hopes that we'll survive. The traditional tales of sharing your food with strangers (remember the colonists and the Native Americans) perhaps have the same sense of propitiation, of buying off the forces of darkness. In the original Thanksgiving, I imagine each group felt it was propitiating the strange other. Thus it's always nice, in a magical sort of way, to have a stranger at the Thanksgiving table. Since I now have teenage children, they and their friends can sometimes serve as the strangers for me and my friends, and we as the strangers for them.

Harvest and joy for some is death and sadness for others (most obviously, of course, for the turkeys). My father died on Thanksgiving Day, and on that not-so-festive Thanksgiving Day I walked along Aquatic Park and found an uprooted evergreen tree. I took it home and planted it outside my apartment. It grew and reached the age of seven. Last Thanksgiving, having moved, I drove by the old apartment building and saw that my father's tree had been cut down. I assume my former upstairs neighbors were motivated by hatred of life and desire for firewood. In the dark of the year, we kill creatures, we cut trees, we harvest.

In the dark of the year, we also light lights. Thus it is in the dark of the year that the Jews celebrate Hanukkah. The lighting of the candles on the menorah, a symbolic tree, parallels the well-known tree with lights in that other solstice celebration, Christmas. Each tradition suggests growth and light in a time of death and darkness.

The proximity of Christmas to the solstice does make it astronomically very close to a real new year's festival. Now, Jesus Christ was not born on December 25th (Jung thought Jesus was really a Gemini). December 25th is a date taken from an old Mithraic festival celebrating the birth of the new light (the sun, reborn at the winter solstice). Out of the darkness the divine child, the light, is born. Similarly, the Eleusinian mysteries of Greece (which are still, unfortunately, mysteries) seem to have involved a celebration of the new light, seen as a newborn child, Iacchos (another name for Dionysus). Christian writers often considered Dionysus one with the Devil, so the new life (baby Dionysus), born on the darkest day of the year, might relate equally well to Lucifer (which means light-bearing) as to Christ.

And now is the time—why, you will see soon enough—for an old Estonian fairy tale.

Once upon a time, between Christmas and New Year's, there was a man who went out partying. He left one party to walk to another. It was late, it was snowing, and he was very drunk, so not surprisingly he got lost. He lay down in the snow under a juniper bush to sleep, waking up to find himself being poked with a pine staff by a tall man dressed in white. "Who are you?" the tall man asked. "Long Hans," the drunk replied, waking up.

"Wake up, you silly man, Long Hans, wake up. Don't you know that if you sleep here you'll surely die?" And the tall man helped him up and led him through the deep snow, parting it with his staff (just like Good King Wenceslas!) until they came to a clearing where there were two other men, also dressed in white, sitting around a fire. For thirty feet around the fire there was no snow on the ground, but Hans, still cold from lying in the snow, leaned close to the fire and drank a warm drink as the men talked in a strange language. He drank several more warm and intoxicating drinks, fell asleep, and in the morning, waking up, found himself alone with a terrible hangover. At first he assumed the loud pounding he heard was in his head, but walking a little bit he came upon a cave, from which the sounds obviously came. He entered and saw a great fire and numerous incredibly strong dwarfs (dressed, because of the intense heat, only in aprons), working away at hammers, anvils, and bellows, pausing occasionally only to drink some water. Seated and giving directions with hand signals was the man with the pinewood staff, dressed no longer in white, but in black. Hans watched them work for several hours, and only when they flung aside their hammers and marched out of the cave did the master speak to Hans.

"I'm sorry I couldn't speak to you sooner, but we were, as you could see, very busy. But now you must be my guest and see how we live. Wait here while I change out of these dirty clothes." And he unlocked a door and led Hans through to a sparkling treasure chamber. Everywhere, gold and silver bars lay sparkling, and Hans, amazed, began to count them, until the man laughed at him: "Oh, stop counting or you'll never finish. If you're so fascinated, why don't you take one of these bars as a present?"

But try as Hans might, he couldn't lift a bar. "If you're that weak," the man laughed again, "you'll have to settle for just looking at them." And so he led Hans through his domain, from one room to the next, each filled with gold and silver, until finally Hans could restrain himself no longer and asked, "Why do you hoard all this treasure down here under the earth, where it will do no one any good? If you'd share these riches with the people, everyone would be rich, and no one would need to work or suffer."

"And that is exactly why," he answered, "I keep these riches away from people. Without labor, the world be idle; only through work and suffering can people ever accomplish anything."

But Hans still protested at how pointless and greedy it was that these riches should do no one any good, and yet still the owner of it should struggle to increase his riches each day.

"But I am not really a man," his host replied, "though I take that shape now. I am really one of the beings to whom is given care of the world. I and my workers mine the gold and silver under the earth, making sure a small portion of it finds its way every year to the upper world, to help the world carry on its business. But we make sure it is only through hard work and patience, or through luck, that riches come, for we dig out the gold and silver and then mix it with dirt and rock and sand. But now I must change for dinner."

Hans couldn't believe his eyes when the man returned. He was dressed in the finest flame-red silk garments, with a gold belt and a golden crown, and carried a golden staff. They went to another room for dinner, where the dwarfs served them delicious food, sometimes leaping upon the table to fill a goblet or bring a new dish. Hans drank and ate and listened as the man in the flame-colored suit told him of his life.

"Between Christmas and New Year's," he said, "I like to visit the earth, but I must admit people don't impress me very much, always fighting and complaining of others, never acknowledging their own sins."

Hans wanted to deny this, but he couldn't, so he had another drink and found himself drifting to sleep. He had wonderful dreams, of the gold bars and being able to lift them, of the blacksmiths busily working, sparks flying before his eyes. But when he awoke he was in the woods, and instead of the warmth of the underworld fire he was basking in the warmth of the sunlight.

He looked around at the summer day and concluded that he must be mad, or he must have dreamed the whole thing. But in front of him were the remains of a fire, and, peeking closely, he saw that the ashes were really silverdust, and the half-burnt log was made of gold. Quickly he took off his winter coat and gathered up the ashes and the log in it.

Thus Hans became rich. But he knew his neighbors would ask embarrassing questions, so he moved to a distant area, bought a home, married a pretty woman with whom he lived richly and well. And he had some children to whom, on his deathbed, he told this story of how he had been made rich by the Lord of the Underworld.

The punch line tells what you may have figured out already: Hans had been made rich by the Devil. (Maybe all very rich men are in some sense made rich by the Devil. Hans wisely moves so that he doesn't have to admit this source of his money.) Lord of the Underworld, dressed in flame red, making life tough for people, custodian of money—this is plainly the Devil, although in this folktale as in rock and roll, there is a certain sympathy. But when I first heard this story, I was struck with the similarity between the Devil and Santa Claus. In the folktale, the Devil appears in this world during the holiday season, is associated with fire and heat as well as with cold and winter, carries a pinewood staff, dresses in a flame-red suit, has dwarf assistants, and gives the man a wonderful gift.

We call him St. Nick, others call him Old Nick. They both wear that red suit, and both come from the cold place. Both have curious associations with fire (Santa comes down the chimney); both are agents of divine justice (he's gonna find out who's naughty or nice). Unlike God, Santa has a Mrs. Claus waiting for him at home. And in folklore the Devil, too, usually has a female companion, his grandmother and/or wife, at home. They both have numerous little assistants. *Santa* is an anagram for *Satan*. And Santa is even associated with horned creatures (reindeer). He probably wears that red hat in order to hide his own horns.

Unfortunately, neither I nor Jerry Falwell get the credit for first suggesting Santa's iconographic similarity to Satan. The credit, I believe, belongs to that student of theosophy and son-in-law of a famous suffragette, L. Frank Baum. The villain in both *Ozma of Oz* and *The Emerald City of Oz*, is the evil Nome King, sometimes called Roquat the Red. His body is round as a ball (In what Baum wished to be the last in the Oz series, he leads his nomes to attack Oz from their vast network of underground caverns. When (in *Ozma*) Dorothy first meets this little fat man, she exclaims, "Why, he looks just like Santa Claus!" This leads the underworld monarch to quote, "He had a red face and a round little belly / That shook when he laughed like a bowl full of jelly." And all notice that when he laughs, he really does shake like a bowl full of jelly.

If you'd have asked Christians of the past to comment on a man dressed in red who flies through the sky in a chariot pulled by horned creatures, comes down the chimney, and gives children too much stuff (so that Christmas has nothing whatsoever to do with the contemplation of Christ), they would, of course, have identified him as the Devil. The central issue of Christmas is what did you get; the goal is somehow, out of the darkness, to get riches. Santa, like the Devil, is the god of materialism. It is fitting that, living in the age of the anti-Christ as we do, with such a focus on material goods, the Satan Claus myth should flourish, that the celebration of Christmas exceed all rational and puritan bounds.

I, a thoroughly modern man, am delighted with Santa. During the dark time of the year, I lie to my little girl and tell her of this strange man who will bring her toys. (I am no doubt encouraging her to be pagan, to believe in such local and minor deities.) And, of course, in a crucial ritual, parents give Santa gifts, too, to propitiate him. I usually leave cookies and brandy (cognac, if I can afford it) on the mantle. In Santa we celebrate the positive side of the Devil.

New Year's Eve announces the last of the new year festivals. Here the ritual is clear: a party, with drinking. When I was growing up, my father had a friend who was, I suppose, an alcoholic. He had nothing but disdain for New Year's Eve, calling it "amateur night." It was the one night of the year he stayed home and got sober.

For the rest of us, New Year's Eve is the night to get drunk. The party always starts late and, it seems to me, slow. We know the old year is in its death throes, and the party tries to die with it. But midnight is a release. We scream and celebrate, as if to say, "I never really liked you at all, old year. I was just faking it! You were terrible, really. You promised a lot, but you didn't come through. I love the new year, not you, old year—I'm glad you're dead." And suddenly, the year, the darkness, seems to be over. I kiss. I eat my herring (an old Norwegian custom—eat herring at midnight on New Year's Eve and you'll have money all year long). I feel hope.

We sing, play instruments, set off fireworks (some shoot guns). The noise is part of the ritual. On New Year's Eve the evil spirits are about (just as they are on the Celtic new year's eve, Halloween). By making noise, we scare off the evil spirits and so have license to be wild. Since the evil spirits are gone, nothing will be taken the wrong way, all our post-midnight actions will be just good fun.

And the next day, a hangover or, if you're lucky, another party. I always go to my friend's mother's house for saki and Japanese food and football games. And then the long-awaited emptiness of real winter.

Emily Dickinson wrote:

> There's a certain Slant of light,
> Winter Afternoons—
> That oppresses, like the Heft
> Of Cathedral Tunes—
>
> Heavenly Hurt, it gives us—
> We can find no scar
> But internal difference,
> Where the meanings are.

There is in winter that wonderful quality of light. While it is still a time for despair, for me it all becomes clear with the light. The meaning may be more musical than rational, but with that beautiful light of a winter afternoon, I do feel meaning in it all. We'll have the long quiet days, days without holidays and parties, to feel the internal difference, to feel how, out of the new year, there might grow a new you, a new me.

Reference

Dickinson, E. *The Complete Poems of Emily Dickinson*, Thomas H. Johnson, ed. Boston: Little, Brown and Co., 1960.

In the Palm of My Hand

I HAD A BREAK IN MY LIFE LINE, so I was always afraid to get my palm read. After all, who want to hear the bad news? But then my life line joined together—yes, the lines in your hand do change. My life seemed to have gotten pretty together, too. So, fairly confident that my imminent death wouldn't be predicted, I went the week after Palm Sunday looking for palm readings.

In the phone book, palm readers are listed under spiritualists. Most all of them offered a combination of services, a psychic reading as well as a palm reading. I figured I was like the weirdo who asks for straight sex at an exotic whorehouse; I wanted a plain old palm job, but most of the artistes seemed likely to throw in a psychic reading whether I wanted it or not. I'd just have to take my chances.

So on Monday I drove in Oakland for a psychic-and-palm reading. After sitting in my parked car for a minute, calming myself, I walked up the stairs of Madam Jackson's white stucco house. I rang the bell, but no one was there. So I drove to a palm reader deeper in Oakland. No one was there. Then I drove over to a reader in Albany. No one was there either. Somehow I had expected these psychics to know that I, a paying customer, was coming. But even with psychics, you need to call first.

On Tuesday I decided to proceed more rationally. I went to Shambhala (an occult bookstore) and asked them to recommend a palm reader. They knew of no palm readers, except a guy who sometimes works on Telegraph Avenue. They did have two directories of services and resources—lots of astrologers, numerologists, tarot readers, psychics, and Eastern teachers—but there wasn't one palm reader.

At Cody's Bookstore, the guy in charge of the occult section told me he thought palmistry wasn't very popular in the new age because it had an intellectual content. After all, it is much easier simply to channel. With palmistry, you have to learn and actually remember what the lines represent. You can't really do it on pure intuition. He also suggested that most of the old-style palmists would probably give pretty stock readings: "I see a boy in a field," etc., and would base their readings on clues they would pick up from me.

Finally a woman at Lewin's Metaphysical Bookstore was able to recommend a palmist named Lynda Tish. I immediately called for an appointment but got a message machine. Fearful that I might never get a palm reading in the Bay Area, I went back to the yellow pages, which list ten or so palm readers, most of them madame someone or another. I called Madame Jackson and got a price—$20.00—and an appointment.

Madame Jackson was a older lady, dark and vaguely exotic, with large gold earrings. She preferred that I didn't tape the reading (it would obviously disturb her psychic sensitivity). I sat down at her white table in her very white house, extending my hands as directed. She told me to make a wish. (I didn't ask if my wish would be granted—it was nice just to be given a wish.) Then she warned me, in an obvious set speech, that she'd tell me the good and the bad, "*Whatever* I see, okay?" I nodded.

Generally the news was good. She saw that I'd live to be eighty-seven (what a life line!) and I'd have good luck with an upcoming large purchase, that I've traveled a lot and there would be more traveling in my future. I could believe all this. She also told me I should stay with my music, that music could be a career sideline for me. I was delighted at this vision, and although I don't find it likely, it is possible; I do play the piano, have written songs, and once even received the fruitless honor of having a demo played for Cyndi Lauper's people.

Then she saw (she never just thought, she always *saw*) some problem in my love life, some misunderstanding. I saw no problems in my love life except my wife's hay fever, but Madame Jackson assured me not to worry, the problems would work out. I suddenly began to figure that she expected me to have some sort of problem, that she was sort of searching for why I came here, for what my problem was. Undoubtedly, most of her clients have definite problems they want help with. I started wondering if maybe I should tell her right away that I was here mostly to do an article on palm reading.

But then I heard her say, “I see a dentist.” She looked up at me quizzically. Suddenly I snapped to attention. Oh my god, she sees a dentist—aggh, here’s the bad news: a root canal in my future!

“A dentist?” I whimpered.

She looked at me coldly and enunciated, “A *Dennis*. Is there a Dennis in your life?”

Well, I admitted, I had just the previous night been drinking beer with a Dennis and a couple of other guys I play basketball with, but I couldn’t really see any problem.

“No, no problem with Dennis,” she assured me. “It will work out.”

At the end of the reading, I asked her about herself and about how she had learned to read palms. She told me that she was an Egyptian, born of a psychic family: “I was born knowing how to read palms.” And indeed her palm reading was at least half a psychic reading (she only pointed out one line). She admitted that she was looking at my aura as much as at my palms.

On the way out, I saw that her mantle was full of china bric-a-brac (women of a certain age always seem to accumulate china bric-a-brac). In the middle of the mantle was a tall white china female figure. I suggested this looked like an altar, but her religious bric-a-brac was obviously none of my business. I didn’t mean to pry.

I liked the reading and thought she had a reasonable number of “hits.” It’s nice to have an old Egyptian psychic with big gold earrings tell you you have nothing to worry about and suggest you might still have a career in music. Still, I wanted a genuine *palm* reading. So I drove down Telegraph Avenue and found the street palmist. The long-haired young man, Michael Schemel, told me he charged on a sliding scale, ten to twenty dollars, and I sat down.

First he meditated, “to clear out the previous reading.” Then, to my relief, he seemed to actually read the lines in my hand. He pointed to where my life line crossed another line (x marks the spot) and told me that in three or five years a big change was possible. He saw two roads, “one is the conservative easy way, the other is doing all the exciting things you want to do, going for the gusto.” For some, a beer commercial quote in a spiritual reading might seem a bit distracting, but for me sitting there on Telegraph Avenue, it seemed appropriate, even charming.

Like Madame Jackson, he said I had traveled a lot and would travel more. He said I was intuitive (this is true) and that people at work take advantage of me. Of course, this is true, although this is probably the case for everyone: why do you think they call it work? He told me I had two kids (I have three, although men can never be sure), that I was very receptive to outside influences (I am), and that there were three or four major things for me to master in life. I wish he'd told me what they were.

On Wednesday, I interviewed a Jungian analyst with an interest in palmistry, Wayne Detloff, M.D. I suggested that the lines of the hands represented what Jung called the archetypes. Detloff agreed, explaining that he thought of them as "kind of a visible interface between things that are more psychological and things that are more physical."

While he doesn't use palmistry very much with his patients, he did say that his knowledge of the hands is very much part of him and that he always pays attention to people's hands and gestures. People learn to disguise their faces, he explained, but they remain unconscious of what their hands communicate.

Detloff explained that he was originally a clinical psychologist and then became a medical doctor. "During my medical training, whenever I did physicals, I would always take at least a quick glance at the hands; it's amazing what you can get in a very short time," he said.

While Detloff has read, indeed collects, traditional palmistry books, he seemed more interested in dermatoglyphics (skin markings), a field primarily researched by anthropologists and geneticists. He told me that geneticists, researching the fine lines of the hand, have found thirty or so medical syndromes that have anatomical concomitants in the hands. These syndromes are either genetic or caused by something going wrong early in gestation. The fine lines of the hands are actively formed in the first trimester, and so they reflect crucial disturbances in fetal progress during this period. The most well known example is perhaps Down's syndrome, which shows a characteristic hand line formation.

Detloff seemed astounded that people could still so consistently ignore the genetic factor in the psyche (Jung's archetypes). A serious palmistry, united with the scientific discipline of dermatoglyphics, would perhaps be a way of understanding an individual's genetically determined psychological predispositions.

There is a small tradition of Jungian interest in palmistry. Jung himself wrote an introduction to Julius Spier's *The Hands of Children*. And Detloff's serious interest in palmistry was sparked by his own work with a student of Spier's, Kate Marcus, Ph.D. While Dr. Detloff admitted that hand interpretation demands intuition—many palmists, including Kate Marcus, have also been psychics—he pointed out that many arts, including dream interpretation and interviewing, require intuition. Detloff insisted that there are objective features to be found in the hands. He said, for example, that he can usually do a pretty good guess of people's psychological types (thinking, feeling, intuition, or sensation) from looking at their palms. I, of course, wanted a quick Jungian reading of my palm, but this seemed inappropriate, like asking for a parlor trick instead of deep analysis. I did get one practical tip from Detloff: the greater the difference between the two hands, the greater the complexity of the individual, and the more opposites for this individual to integrate within his or her personality.

The next day, I went into San Francisco to get some books and articles on palmistry, including some books by Charlotte Wolff, a medical doctor, Ph.D., refugee from Hitler, lesbian activist, and legendary palm reader. In one of Wolff's two autobiographies, she recounts a fascinating reading she gave Virginia Woolf—a much richer story than the account by the famous palm reader Cheiro of his Mark Twain reading, a reading which Cheiro claimed inspired Twain's book, *Pudd'nhead Wilson*.

Since I was in the city anyway, I stopped by the financial district, where I had previously seen a small palm reading sign in a second-floor window. I was interested in checking out someone who gave palm readings to stockbrokers and bankers.

I parked in an expensive garage and walked upstairs to find two attractive women in their twenties and a small child in a walker. An AM rock and roll station played loudly in the background.

"How much is a palm reading?" I asked.

"Who sent you?" one of the women replied.

"I just saw the sign," I said.

"Fifteen dollars. Sit down."

I sat down on the couch, next to the AM radio blaring Roberta Flack's "Killing Me Softly." One of the women sat next to me while the other disappeared into a back room. The "reader" told me I had two wishes and to tell her one—a good way to learn what to give back to me, I figured. Then she made the standard speech telling me she'd give me the good and the bad and was I ready for that? She sounded like bored salesperson giving an old pitch.

Then she started talking in the vaguest generalities, while the radio blared and the baby babbled and wandered on the floor in front of us: you're a real go-getter (I guess she figured I worked in the area), you get tension headaches (I don't), you have no money problems (absurd!), but you spend more than you make (who doesn't?), you have a problem, you've travelled a lot, etc. She talked for about 10 minutes, told me that she could meditate or light some candles to solve my problems for me (for a price). Then she asked if I had any questions.

"Aren't you going to look at my hands?" I asked.

She looked at me as if I were crazy.

"I asked for a palm reading," I explained, "and you never even asked to see my hands."

"Okay," she shrugged, "whatever you want, but it will be just the same." And it was.

After I left, I sort of wondered what business these two young women were really in, what sort of madame ran *this* palm reading shop. Later a friend of mine told me about going into Chicago's skid row when he was thirteen and passing by a "gypsy" palm reading establishment, with lots of very young women languorously lounging around. Even the little boys knew that palm reading was just the cover story. And I suppose a massage parlor would be inappropriate in the financial district, but a palm reading shop (for a quick noontime palm job) would be a good cover.

That evening I went to see Lynda Tish and finally got a real palm reading, indeed a whole hand reading.

She started by making prints of my hands (Detloff had said that a responsible reader always took a print, in order to see the fine lines). She stared at the prints for a while, mumbling to herself. Then she spoke, pointing out the different kinds of fingers, fingerprints, lines, and other markings on my hands, tying them to my personality. She really studied my hands, recognizing and interpreting where I had dislocated my little finger and repeatedly jammed my thumb playing basketball. And as she spoke, unlike the other palm readers, she actually touched my hands; later she pointed out that she had to feel for temperature and responsiveness.

After I got home, I played the tape for my wife, and she said that she could have picked this reading as mine out of any number of other readings. Indeed, Lynda was so accurate that to summarize what she said would be egotistical as well as boring. One practical tip, though, for you teachers—it helps to have, as I do, large knuckles; these suggest you are analytical, can figure out and thus explain to your students how you do things. Some of the accurate things she said did, of course, agree with some of the accurate things my other readers had said, for example, that I'm intuitive, responsive, well traveled (although Lynda suggested these travels could equally well be inner voyages).

Normally Lynda does a two-hour reading for one hundred dollars. I got a much briefer reading (half an hour) but was still impressed. Of course, if you have pretty good self-knowledge, sharing the truth about yourself may not be worth $100. I've had years of Jungian analysis, so I felt I pretty much already knew what she told me. But still it was useful to be clearly *reminded* about myself.

Lynda has been seriously studying palmistry for thirteen years. Five years ago, however, she consulted a lawyer who said that while she could probably get away with practicing in Berkeley, in most places palmistry was illegal. Primarily so that she could practice palmistry legally (and thus with dignity), Lynda enrolled in a graduate program in career counseling. In 1985, two weeks before her graduate work was completed, the California Supreme Court overturned the bans on astrologers, palmists, and other occult seers. The court's major motivation, Lynda explained, was that they felt these laws were originally put on the books to discriminate against gypsies. The decision said something to the effect that palmists and astrologers had as much right to predict the future as stockbrokers did.

Since Lynda is not a therapist, she does not encourage repeat visits. While the lines of the hand do change over time, it takes at least six weeks for even a hint of a new line to form. If you want another reading, she says, you should wait at least nine months or a year. She provides her clients with a cassette recording, hand prints, and explanatory handouts, so that they can remember and use their single reading.

She shies away from the predictions typical of traditional palmists, although, as Detloff pointed out to me, any accurate reading of character will suggest kinds of situations in which people will likely find themselves. Like many palmists, she does psychic readings, but she doesn't combine her palm readings with her psychic readings. While she no doubt uses her intuition, her palm readings are based on a systematic and objective reading of the hands.

My sister Margaret once defined for me the correct attitude to take towards the various "occult" arts. If you believe them totally, you are clearly crazy, but if you disbelieve them totally, you are probably also crazy (if a different kind of crazy). All my rational friends had assumed I would test palmistry's accuracy—for example, checking to see if the palmists gave the same readings. But for me, the experience of the readings seemed more relevant than deciding whether to "believe" or not.

Like other "occult" arts, palmistry has a long history, apparently stretching back three thousand years (in China); it was certainly old in Aristotle's time. As Jung pointed out in his preface to Julius Spier's *The Hands of Children: An Introduction to Psycho-chirology*, "the rise of the natural sciences and hence of rationalism in the eighteenth century brought these ancient arts . . . into disrepute." But, Jung went on, "in the twentieth century, after two hundred years of intensive scientific progress, we can risk resurrecting these almost forgotten arts which have lingered on in semi-obscurity and can test them in the light of modern knowledge for possible truths." My week-long experience with palm reading has resurrected this art for me personally. Just as I like knowing the twelve astrological signs, I like knowing the traditional terms from this old if not yet reputable art. Even if I can't quite interpret what they mean, I like knowing my fingers are (from pinky on) Mercury, Apollo, Saturn, Jupiter, and that the thumb represents the ego and has no "archetypal" or planetary associations. I've had my horoscope done, but palmistry does *seem* more objective than astrology. After all, the planets are absurdly far away—clearly way out there. But my hands are obviously a part of me. There are clear terminological correlations with astrology, but with palmistry you don't have to remember (or find!) your horoscope. You just look at your hands.

While a serious palm reader can spend an hour interpreting the lines on one finger, I have only a little lore. I can see, for example, that my fingerprints are of the air (loop), fire (whorl), and water (yin-yang) patterns, that not one of my fingers is of the earth (pyramid) design. And I am not an earthy kind of guy.

Still, my hands say, I can produce in the material world. This is shown by the lines on the third (bottom) phalanges of my fingers. Indeed, Lynda jokingly told me that in a job interview I could just show the interviewer the lines on my third phalange, and the would-be boss would see that I was a person who produced. And despite my unearthy essence, I do make things, this article, for example.

Most of all, of course, it's fun simply to be able to name the lines on my hand. No matter what you believe, the lines of your hand are clearly the lines of *your* hand. And I don't just look at my own hand, of course. Even with my minimal knowledge, I freely look at my friends' hands. I identify the various lines and interpret for them the difference between their right and left hands. For a right hander, the left hand represents what they have been born with, and the right hand represents what they've made out of themselves. It is nice just to have the opportunity to talk with your friends about archetypally important things—head, heart, life, fate. At the very least, you get to hold a lot of hands.

References

Spier, J. *The Hands of Children: An Introduction to Psycho-Chirology*. London: Routledge and Kegan Paul, 1944.

Jung, C. G. 1944. "Foreword to Spier: *The Hands of Children*." In *CW* 20:820–821. Princeton, N.J.: Princeton University Press, 1973.

Don't Dream It, Be It: *The Rocky Horror Picture Show* as Dionysian Revel

EVERY SATURDAY NIGHT, IN THEATERS across the country, groups of people (most of them young) participate in a Dionysian revel and ritual. This experience is focused upon a movie, *The Rocky Horror Picture Show* (directed by Jim Sharman, 1975). My daughter Jenny is one of the regular bacchants, and I recently went with a group of my friends to see her perform. Some of my friends were curious about how I felt seeing my daughter in undies and garter belt, playing Frank-N-Furter, mad scientist, bisexual, cannibal, and leader of a pack of perverts.

Well, I felt just like a father watching his daughter in a school play: Proud Poppa. I write this essay, in part, to explain why I felt that way.

You should understand, those of you who have never been to *Rocky* (you've labeled "virgins" by the cognoscenti), that the movie demands audience involvement. So a cast, with meticulously exact costuming and props, acts out the movie in front of the screen, miming the movements of the actors. Members of the audience continually shout at the move screen, anticipating lines and action, roaring witticisms (usually obscene), and commenting on the characters (for example, shouting "asshole" in unison whenever Brad, the straight lead, appears on the screen). And at one point, large portions of the audience join the cast in doing the Time Warp, dancing in the aisles. There are people who, with an almost religious devotion, participate in this ritual every Saturday night, week after week, month after month, even year after year.

This movie in particular has become a cult film in large part because, like Dionysian ritual, it demands audience involvement. After all, the most obvious moral in the movie is, "Don't dream it, be it."

Nietzsche contrasted Apollonian dreaming with Dionysian intoxication. Jung, in analyzing Nietzsche's psychological type, argues that Nietzsche's Dionysus represented extraverted sensation, while his Apollo represented introverted intuition. Obviously, the participants in the *Rocky* revel are not passively, introvertedly dreaming but are actively, extravertedly being. And certainly the *Rocky* revelers are intoxicated, although not all of them with booze and drugs. The *Rocky* experience is one of extraverted sensation: get in the aisles and do it. Don't watch the movie, be the movie.

The hero of the movie, Frank (astoundingly well played by Tim Curry), is in several obvious but interesting ways like Dionysus. They are both, as we shall see, associated with intoxication, dancing, madness, transvestism, love and sex, extremes of pleasure and suffering, murder and dismemberment, grotesque eating rituals, and frenzy, and moisture.

Near the beginning of the movie, a nice young couple (Brad and Janet) run out of gas on a dark and stormy night. They go to a nearby castle to ask for help and find Frank and his revelers drinking and dancing. As host of the party, encouraging drinking, dancing, and dissolution, Frank (like many another party host) acts a Dionysian role. Frank is a bizarre transvestite who, later in the movie, will get involved sexually with both Brad and Janet. And Dionysus was frequently referred to as "womanish" or "man-womanly." (In *The Bacchae*, Dionysus caused the too rational and uptight Pentheus to go around in drag before finally being torn to pieces by a group of wild women, including his own mother.)

Dionysus is the mad god, and Frank embodies madness. Frank-N-Furter, like his prototype, Dr. Frankenstein, is a mad scientist who has discovered the secret of life itself. But he creates not a monster, but a muscle man, the beautiful Rocky. Later Frank falls into a rage at the intrusion of his old lover, Eddie, and he hacks Eddie to pieces with a pickax. Dionysus is mythologically and ritually associated with death by dismemberment. He is the twice-born god; after being murdered and dismembered, he is miraculously brought back to life (thus the secret of creation of life out of death belongs to Dionysus). And when Frank serves Eddie's flesh for dinner, he is almost following a Dionysian tradition (the eating of the raw flesh of a bull—symbolically Dionysus himself—was part of some Dionysian rituals).

Dionysus was *Liber*, was freedom. Repressed Greek women were attracted to Dionysian religion's promise of freedom. Dionysus called, "Leave your looms and go boogie in the woods all night long." On most Saturday nights, my two-year-old (Lily) will ask me where her sister Jenny is. Even though it is well before midnight at such times, I can't help answering with my favorite weekly sentence: "Jenny's dancing at the movies." I do have a patriarchal side, but I also feel that it's wonderful for someone who's a week-daily prisoner of the ninth grade to break free, to dance Saturdays after midnight at the movies. *Rocky* breaks down traditional barriers, allowing people to shout obscenities in a crowded theater, to dress outlandishly (and cross-sexually), to leave their seats and dance at the movies. Dionysus was *Lysis*, the loosener. And Frank loosens up Brad and Janet, just as people go to *Rocky* to get loose, to have a good time.

Jane Harrison argues that the essence of Dionysian religion was that the worshiper could become the god (no one could become Zeus or Apollo). Frank, too has his gods, his idol; as a transvestite, he is living out his identification with such luminaries as Lili St. Cyr and Fay Wray. Near the end of the movie Frank sings, "Whatever Happened to Fay Wray?" He's joined by four others, including Brad and Janet, who join him in song and orgy. At this point, Frank's former servants enter and tell him that they are now in charge (perhaps, it is implied, they have received word from the home planet of Transexual, in the galaxy of Transylvania). They tell Frank (as many followers of Dionysus have been told), "Your lifestyle's too extreme!" The servants will return to their home planet, but first they shoot Frank with a laser. Rocky, his beloved muscleman, picks up the dead body and, impervious to the laser attack, starts ascending a conveniently located RKO tower. Thus Frank finally becomes Fay Wray (in the arms of his King Kong) and lives out his tragic but heroic fantasy.

Don't dream it, be it. Thus the movie *Rocky* has encouraged people to act out their identifications with the movie's characters. And traditionally the Dionysian is associated with the mask and with drama. Walter Otto writes, near the end of his moving book on Dionysus:

> The wearer of the mask is seized by the sublimity and divinity of those who are no more. He is himself and yet someone else. Madness has touched him – something of the mystery of the mad god, something of the spirit of the mad god who lives in the mask and whose most recent descendant is the actor. (p. 210)

So my daughter is in essence an actor. Acting is a rather crazy thing to do, but Dionysus teaches (according to Otto) that madness is a companion to life at its healthiest. Hamlet imaged acting as being "mad in craft," and for an actor Dionysian madness is tempered with Apollonian craft (discipline). Those who ritualized the Dionysian madness, who assimilated it to Apollo's schedule at Delphi, knew that a regulated ecstasy lost some of its danger. So instead of everyone becoming possessed by the spirit of the god, the select few (priests/actors) enacted the possession for the group as a whole. At *Rocky* a select cast does perform in front of the screen. And to add to the ritual feeling, much of the audience participates, too, shouting at the screen like a chorus in a Greek drama or the respondents at a revival meeting. Dionysus was *Bromios*, the roarer, and the audience enjoys the freedom of yelling itself hoarse.

Behind a Dionysian ritual there is often an Apollonian structure. Thus, an intellectual criminologist frames the movie, narrates the story. And the cast for *Rocky* is a theater group; people have to show up every Saturday night, know their parts, pay dues, clean up, etc. And the Dionysian message of the movie – don't dream it, be it – is tempered with an Apollonian moral – lifestyles can be too extreme.

Let me end with a plug. Every Saturday at midnight, at the U. C. Theater on University Avenue in Berkeley, *The Rocky Horror Picture Show* is playing. The cast, suitably named Indecent Exposures, is (I am told by my daughter and her friends) one of the best in the country. It is a terrific movie, a Dionysian revel/ritual, and an unforgettable experience. If you don't want to be it, at least see it.

Reference

Otto, W. *Dionysus: Myth and Cult*. Bloomington, Ind.: Indiana University Press, 1965.

Marie-Louise von Franz and *The Way of the Dream*

In San Francisco at the Palace of Fine Arts this weekend, a thousand people each paid $150 to see a ten-hour documentary film series featuring Marie-Louise von Franz interpreting dreams. The twenty half-hour films (five hours on men's dreams and five hours on women's) showed the actual dreamers telling their dreams (always in visually interesting locations, such as an odd apartment, by the ocean, or under an ancient arch), then von Franz giving her dream interpretations. At the end of the weekend, we all understood why people at the Jung Institute in Zurich nicknamed her "Marvelous."

At appropriate intervals, our moderator, James Hall (a Jungian analyst from Dallas) would offer brief remarks and take questions and comments. Fraser Boa, the film's producer, director, narrator, and on-screen interviewer of von Franz, was there as well and occasionally offered his comments. The real thrill for me was to spend an intense cinematic weekend with Marie-Louise von Franz, the smartest person in the world as far as I'm concerned.

Because I'd studied her work for years, I relished the smallest personal details the films revealed, like the curious fact that she was wearing two watches, that her bookcase was messy (like mine), with books stuck in on top of other books. She had an English bulldog at her feet much of the time, a picture of another English bulldog over her desk, and dirt under her fingernails. I was most of all impressed by the force of her personality. In one of the films, she did a marvelous bit—sometimes she was like a comedian "doing bits"—on her different personalities, her different complexes: sometimes she is just an old peasant woman with nothing in her mind but what's on the table, but sometimes she is a scholar of ancient languages, or a psychologist helping people, or a mischievous little boy. She said she could name many other people she sometimes was: certainly one of them is the weird old wise woman—at one point, she took off her glasses and talked into the camera, and I thought, "*Oh yeah*, anything you say, old wise woman." The trick of handling your complexes, she explained, is to be *conscious* about moving from one personality to another. She said she knows how to let the mischievous little boy out and have a lot of fun, but she also knows when it's time to send him back. This combination of openness and control seems to me a function of maturity: not to eliminate the richness of your personalities (your complexes) but to have some kind of control over their entrances and exits (each one of us, every day, plays many parts, acts many ages).

Hall was the perfect moderator for the weekend: relaxed and funny but also with his own wisdom about the way of the dream. In his opening remarks, he told how he'd once been part of a big weekend (on parapsychology, I think) and had done, he thought, very well. Then he dreamed he'd been masturbating in public. "At least I've got this big podium here," he said, setting a light tone. I especially enjoyed how he referred to his "alleged mother complex." At the beginning of the second day, he told his dream from the night before. He'd been approaching a door labeled VUTS, which he knew stood for Von Franz Unresolved Transference Society. Inside, he expected only a few besides himself (including Fraser Boa); instead it was a huge hall, full of people talking about von Franz's two watches, wanting souvenir jars of dirt from her garden, wondering if it was a barometer or a stuck clock on the wall in her office. Most of the crowd at the film series weren't carrying the torch for von Franz that I was (some had never heard of her, had just come out of interest in dreams), but surely there were a number of us who belonged in VUTS.

I never did find out if it was a barometer or not, but many of my other questions were answered. She had dirt under her fingernails for most of the films not because she's particularly dirty, but because whenever they were not filming, she'd go out to work in her garden—a sensible way to deal with a film crew in her house. She wore two watches, Boa explained, because she'd been on the phone to Los Angeles. Since the films were sometimes spliced together, it was wonderful to see her, in the twinkling of a question, shift from two-watch'd to one-watch'd. While I heard one woman in the crowd characterize von Franz as "dowdy," and while Hall said he thought she often sat and talked like a truck driver, I thought she looked wonderful (she had a *lovely* string of pearls worn directly next to her skin; over the years skin contact does give pearls a special luster).

She was filmed in two separate two-week sessions. Before the filming, she had asked Boa to send her the transcripts of the people telling their dreams. They sent these four months or so before they came to see her. "Where shall we begin?" she asked, when they showed up. "Well, with the first dream, of course," they stammered. "Oh yes," she said and reached for the envelope with the transcripts, which she then opened for the first time. She wanted her responses to be from the unconscious, not thought out. She wanted to do what she does in analysis, hear a dream and then interpret it. Boa filmed her for two weeks and went home to Canada to get the film processed, where most of it broke and was destroyed in one of the baths you give film to develop it. Boa called von Franz up to tell her, but she wasn't really interested in reshooting it; nor apparently was Boa (his cameraman was off on another project, for one thing). But then, to use Boa's phrase, "filthy lucre" saved the project. The insurance companies would pay for a reshoot but wouldn't compensate for the loss of the whole project. So Boa used all his powers of persuasion to convince von Franz to go through being filmed again. Boa claimed this reshooting was all for the best—he was able to ask better questions, having prepared himself by listening to the audio of the tapes (which, unlike most of the videos, hadn't been lost). It was during the first filming that she wore two watches, and she does seem a little more vital and spontaneous then.

In order to get a discount ticket, I worked the weekend as one of the ushers, duly authorized by a yellow ribbon tied around my arm. In one film, von Franz referred to the *Cours d'Amours* and the beginnings of love, with knights dedicating themselves to their mistresses. I thought of the knights who wore their mistresses' kerchiefs on their sleeves (thus the expression "wearing your heart on your sleeve"). Looking at the yellow ribbon I was wearing, I imagined myself a knight in the service of von Franz.

The ushers' biggest problem came in restraining the women's assaults on the men's room. The line for the women's room was ridiculously long, while the men's room (after the first few minutes of a break) was easily accessible. During one of the first breaks, I went to use the men's room, not noticing that a line of women had formed. As I entered, a woman at the door snapped at me. "Back of the line, buddy." Looking at the line Xanthippes behind her, I retreated. Returning some minutes later, I noticed no line outside, went into the bathroom, and found women loitering around, waiting their turn in the stalls. Not really bothered, I turned at a discreet angle and used the urinal. No big deal, I thought, and the women weren't particularly distressed or interested either (maybe I should have been insulted). But several men (usually older men) came up to ushers to complain in outrage—they'd gone into the men's room and there were women in there and they couldn't pee! Something had to be done!

The next day, an usher who cared strongly about the issue (thank God, not me—I'd have resigned my commission first) was assigned to hold the women back at the men's room door. There he was, arguing with a woman at the front of the line, who couldn't understand why the men got to go first. "Well, it is the men's room," he explained. This seemed to calm her just a bit, and she was willing to be held back from waiting directly behind the urinals. Finally, when the first flush of men had finished, the women were allowed in. This system worked fairly well, although at slow periods with the door unguarded, both sexes shared the room.

On Sunday, in the films discussing women's dreams, a woman told one dream with exceptional emotion. In the dream, a man had burst into the ladies' room. A close-up showed her horror as she exclaimed: "And there was a MAN in the ladies' room!" Much of the audience broke into laughter: this dream, and von Franz's subsequent discussion of it, echoed so much of what we had been experiencing. Von Franz explained that peeing generally represented "genuine self-expression." Other instincts can be repressed; one can do without sex and for extended periods of time, without eating or sleeping, but peeing cannot be repressed for very long—when you gotta go, you gotta go. In the woman's dream as von Franz interpreted it, it had been her animus interfering with her own genuine self-expression. In the movie house that weekend, we had been playing out a similar problem, with the women feeling that the men were interfering with their genuine self-expression, and the men feeling the women were interfering with their genuine self-expression. And the fault was mostly in the architecture, in the world we were living in, which provided us with comfortable chairs, coffee and croissants, but not enough room for everyone to genuinely express themselves.

I guess part of the problem is also anatomical. Men in general do pee more quickly than women (I hope this comment is seen not as sexism but as statistics). Part of reason is that men are by and large less genteel and more extraverted (in their urination as in other forms of self-expression). So a men's room is a public place, with men lined up next to each other, pissing into a public trough. Women are by and large expected to be more genteel and less extraverted (in their urination as in other forms of self-expression). So women's rooms usually have separate stalls, which offer a woman, even in urination, a longer and more introverted moment for this symbolic for of "self-expression."

Von Franz repeatedly discussed the situation of the animus interfering with women's genuine self-expression. She told the story of how one night she had dreamed of some men breaking into her bedroom, but she didn't know where that dream had come from until she realized that the day before she'd had the thought, about the book she was working on, "This is all nonsense. I should just throw it all away." Realizing this was the critical voice of the negative animus, she could think, "This voice isn't me. I don't think my work is worthless; this in an intruder, to be kept out." And so she went on with her work.

She talked a lot about man/woman fights and offered a vivid image of the woman who cried—"Oh, I'm just a little girl, don't be so mean, so rough to me"—all the while using her animus like a weapon to attack and belittle the man. It's as if the animus is a gangster who has a gun and shields himself from attack by holding this little girl in front of him!

At one point, the film's narrator, Fraser Boa, asked von Franz to comment on the fact that in man/woman arguments, the man sometimes has the fantasy of raping the woman. Astoundingly (and to the consternation of some of the women in the audience), she said this sometimes was a healthy fantasy, because it expressed the man's desire to put the woman in a more female position. When the woman is arguing through her animus, the husband naturally wonders where his wife has gone, the man wonders what happened to the woman. Of course, it's better to think in terms of making love to the woman in order to break her animus feeling, and von Franz said she'd never advise a man to indulge in a rape fantasy, but there is a way in which such a fantasy can arise in a man just because the man wants the woman and not her animus in the argument.

The anima or animus is not only intriguing or inspiring; it can also be repellent or destructive. Hall told how he had, in active imagination, some kind of mythological figure who would give him advice, always very good advice. Once, having had a difficult analytic session (von Franz had rather savagely criticized him), this figure advised him to kill von Franz. "This put me in an ethical dilemma," Hall asserted, for "it's a cardinal rule in active imagination that you don't do anything you wouldn't do in real life." Well, he approached von Franz (in imagination) with some kind of weapon, and she immediately transformed into an eagle and flew away. In the next real analytic session, he had told her this fantasy, and she simply said, "Oh that eagle's my animus. You can kill that."

I think that Jung, too, although getting in touch with the unconscious through the anima, never totally trusted her, never took her as a part of his personality, always experienced her as other (most of us aren't complete psychic androgynes). And while the animus does give a spiritual intellectual depth to women (my own wife, without an animus, could have turned out to be the wandering Jew of the shopping malls, eternally sunk into the world of the feminine, the world of thingness, of shopping and laundry), the animus is not the woman, just as the anima is not the man. When von Franz was nasty to Hall, that was her animus—and when he realized this (and that she'd just as soon, in that situation, have her animus killed), he could relate to her better.

One of Jung's most useful discoveries was that a relationship between a man and a woman inevitably involves a foursome: the man and his anima and the woman and her animus. I know from experience how a woman's animus can throw me into a foul humor, can throw me into the negative anima. I think Samson with Delilah portrays the perfect image of such an anima-possessed man: Samson, the strong man in agony, having lost his power—Delilah cut his hair, the bitch!—and having been chained to a column, is filled with self-pity and eventual rage and violence. So he finally just destroys the whole temple.

The movies frequently helped me better understand the psychological differences between men and women. So often the sexes seem not to understand each other. Just the other day, trying to be nasty to my wife in conversation, I remarked that I found it best to talk to women just as you would talk to plants or dogs; if you *pretend* they can understand, they respond ever so much better. To my surprise, she didn't bat an eye or a husband, but instead smiled in instant agreement: "But that's exactly how I feel about men!"

What von Franz said about men rang true, and for me it was often like being reminded of something I knew but had forgotten, like how men are often in love with love rather than in love with women, or about how Oedipus was, in such a typically masculine way, being *too clever* with his superficial solution to the Sphinx's riddle.

But what she said about women often clarified mysteries for me. Von Franz spoke as if a woman would be somehow odd to want to give up certain household jobs (like doing the laundry), this time of being able to think about her dreams, to be alone for a while, indulging in her love affair with matter. Women do have a love of matter, she said. Laundry and doing the dishes (making things clean) express this love. I was immediately convinced of something I had never made conscious: my wife, Judy, often enjoys being alone with the dishes or the laundry. Of course, she hates picking up other people's objects off the floor and doing various other onerous household tasks. But now, after dinner or in the middle of the day, when I realize she's been gone for an hour while I'm in a swarm of children, animals, life, I know (and she has admitted) that she really is enjoying it, loving matter, introverted and alone in the kitchen or down in the laundry room. (I've subsequently talked to other women about this. Many of them do hate such household tasks, but a surprising number of them confessed, with a guilt perhaps brought on by feminism, that actually they too liked doing the laundry.)

Von Franz pointed out that American society places a premium on moving—corporations don't want you to develop a loyalty to a certain group of friends, or the individuality that comes from being rooted—and that this constant moving is even more upsetting to women than it is to men. It upsets men, too, eventually, but women especially need their garden, their home, their rhythm. My family moved more or less constantly throughout my childhood, and I think I was less bothered by it than my sisters. I was sort of always moving around anyway (little boys with their constant movement). Certainly my mother paid a higher price for all those moves than my father—once, after we moved from Long Island to California, she renounced making friends and only really made friends again three moves later, when we moved to New Jersey and seemed more permanently settled. I think moving really disoriented my mother, and in rebellion against the constant moving of our childhood (which did bring our father the American dream, corporate success), all of her kids have stayed rooted, hardly moving at all.

Some of the women in the audience were offended with von Franz's answer when she was asked how a woman should respond to a husband having an extramarital affair. I though she was reasonable (and not shocking) when she said the woman shouldn't try to talk like a lawyer (she did some marvelous impressions of the impersonal passive constructions one falls into when speaking with the voice of the collective: "In such situations, one should be forced to make a concrete decision within a certain time frame"). Whenever that voice of the collective (or, in this case, the animus) comes in, real feeling is out. The issue is always to speak out of your real feelings. Love, as she pointed out, has only recently if uneasily been linked with marriage—uniting these two is pioneering work, and there really are no rules, no collective patterns to follow: "what should be done by one in such situations." (I find it interesting that the Puritans were crucially influential in bringing love and marriage together. They insisted the double standard was wrong, that men as well as women should be faithful. So if men weren't going to get to have concubines, then they were damn well going to marry someone they loved!) In some situations, von Franz said she'd advise the wife who really loved the husband who had been hit by Cupid's arrow to treat him as though he had the flu and hope he gets better soon. "Real love heals, makes the other person more him or herself," von Franz said.

In the question-and-answer session following these films, our moderator (Hall) began by saying, "I'd like to apologize for von Franz's sexist language"—and there was a scattering of feminist applause. "She should have said cattleshit instead of bullshit." (Indeed, von Franz has used the word *bullshit*—and beneath the joke, I think, there is a point, for bullshitting is classically a more male vice.) The previous films had obviously been the most controversial, with some audible feminine hisses (it is interesting how women have taken up hissing to express "feminist" sentiments, it being a snakelike sound, harking back to Eden). So this was the most controversial of the brief discussion sessions. My friend (male), with whom I had come, asked the obvious but best question: What should the man do when the woman is having the affair? If he expresses his feelings (what the woman was advised to do), is he being anima possessed? Is he supposed to express the collective opinions, talk in terms of logic, rules, time limits (after all, he can't be animus possessed). Oddly, Boa took this question and simply couldn't understand it, while Hall comically edged behind the curtain, obviously not wanting to answer. At first, Boa asked my friend if he were making a statement, then he misparaphrased the question, completely missing the point—finally, as the crowd forced him to understand, however vaguely, he said that he had asked von Franz this in one of the films that had accidentally been destroyed. But what did she say? he was asked. Again, he was unable to answer.

Obviously, the answer in both cases is to speak from the heart, not from collective opinion. Now, my friend was asking the question in a very serious way—the woman with whom he lived was going to Nepal (again) to see if she *really* was in love with the Sherpa with whom she had an affair the last time she was there. (I assume the Sherpa wants to come to the States—I imagine him, the woman, and my friend all living together in Berkeley in an eighties Noel Coward drawing room comedy.) My friend had sort of been feeling that he ought to "act like a man," to set time limits, to not be home when she gets back, to say, "It's him or me, babe." But the night after the first day of the von Franz movies, he'd dreamed of a boy who was wondering what to do in his relationship with some girl and had read that he "must accept her warts and all." This was one of those dreams which don't need interpretation, which just make the point out of the unconscious: obviously, he at least has to try to accept her warts and all, try to be there when she gets back from Nepal.

During the break, my friend got many notes and comments from women, offering answers to his question. An older woman in back of me had started off by saying, "von Franz is much better on men's dreams than on women's dreams." The funny thing is I felt what she'd said on women's dreams to be the better stuff. It's probably easier to look at the blind spots of the other sex—"She was wonderful discussing everyone else's neuroses, but when she got to mine, she was way off base!"

I was especially struck on Saturday when von Franz talked about where people find their spirituality, how they sometimes find the spirit in a brandy bottle, while the true water of life was in dreams. I thought of the *aquavit* I'd been drinking on Friday night with my friend Victor, which had left me a bit hungover on Saturday. I've written my dreams down for years, but it's so easy to backslide into doing it automatically, not taking them seriously enough. And they really are a lot of whatever spiritual life I have. The movies renewed my resolve to take my dreams and work with them more seriously, not just to write them down, but to live with them.

I could identify when von Franz talked about how slow psychological progress can seem, how people complain about having the same dreams (back in high school, etc.) year after year after year. I too have had the same kinds of dreams for so many years now that sometimes I think my psyche is in re-runs. (The idea of analysis is to speed up one's naturally slow psychological change.) Now that I'm clearly in mid-life, I feel the need, as the statue said to Rilke, to change my life. Hall told an encouraging story: von Franz had left her laundry to be done by some woman, and the woman subsequently became ill, so von Franz went to visit the woman and, while she was there, picked up her laundry. That night von Franz dreamed her mother was saying to her, "Marluce, isn't it just like you to give your laundry to a sick woman!" Like that she was thrown back into the mother complex! If von Franz can be repossessed by those old complexes, I can forgive myself a little more for when I backslide into old patterns. (And I love knowing that von Franz's mother called her Marluce!)

The overall message of the weekend was to remind me that the way of the dream is the way out of these old complexes, is the way to the water of life. The problem, often, is that the ego wants what it wants so strongly, so loudly, that it is easy to ignore the dream's quiet message. One way to start taking dreams more seriously is to try to keep the dream image with you all day.

Of course, *just* to "stay with the image" would be taking the approach advocated by the psychologist James Hillman—as if the image were all. Von Franz explicitly said, as if to Hillman, that you need to discard the image, that the meaning is the important thing. The point of holding the image throughout the day would be to try to get at the meaning. But often, von Franz emphasized, we are blind to the meaning in our own dreams (it is easier to see the mote in your neighbor's eye—just as I found von Franz's discussion of women's dreams more memorable). Jung used to tell his dreams to some guy, a man with no particular psychological acumen, just so he could get some response and then say, "No that's not it," thus finding the meaning. Even if working alone, you need to try to find the meaning, to let the next dream correct you if you're not making the right sense of it.

Sometimes the dream will correct you so clearly that all you can do is surrender to its superior wisdom. In this regard, von Franz told about a patient of hers whom she kept urging to write more, to develop his creative side. He, on the other hand, claimed his problems were sexual, that he wasn't leading a full enough sexual life. Von Franz didn't believe this, for the man had a girlfriend and seemed to her to have quite an active sex life. This argument went on and on between the two of them. Finally, he had a dream that he was being chased across a field by a bull. He barely escaped, leaping over the fence as the bull reared. Looking back, he saw the bull sticking its front feet over the fence, revealing that where its penis should have been was a ballpoint pen! Case dismissed.

Reference

von Franz, Marie-Louise. *The Way of the Dream*. Twenty half-hour films produced and directed by Fraser Boa. Toronto: Windrover Film Ltd., 1965.

Pleasing and Agreeable: An Interview with John Freeman

WHEN I MET JOHN FREEMAN — at a Theta Xi "Faculty Roundup" on the U. C. Davis campus — I immediately recognized him as the man who interviewed Jung in the well-known BBC Face to Face series. He agreed to talk to me at a later date about his interview with Jung but warned me that it had happened thirty years before, so he wasn't sure he really had much to say. I reread the transcript of the interview (in *C. G. Jung Speaking*), which took place in October 1959 when Jung was 83 years old, and arranged to visit him in his office on February 9, 1989. The sign on the wall told me he was a visiting professor of political science.

I began by telling him how important his filmed interview of Jung had been to me as a person "steeped in Jung." He responded graciously, but with a disclaimer.

FREEMAN I know nothing about psychology or about Jung. It was a job I had to do, to go and interview Jung. I did it to the best of my ability, and to my great pleasure, because I'd recognized that he was held in the greatest honor and so on. I found that I actually got on with him. We liked one another and got on very well together, which was absolutely fine, but I still don't feel myself in the least bit qualified to talk about him or his work, because I really don't know about it. Moreover, my memory has become, over time, very fallible.

BOE Your interview was such a success, unlike the Richard Evans one (for the "Houston Films," also recorded in *C. G. Jung Speak-*

ing), for example, partly because you seemed to relate to Jung the human being, not just Jung the psychologist.

FREEMAN Well, I'd just say he was a very, very pleasing and agreeable old gentleman—I mean old you see, because I'm the same sort of age now, but at that time I was much younger than he was. I took to him instantly, and he responded by letting me treat him just as another human being and not making any big deal about it. So we got along excellently well.

BOE Did you choose to interview him, or was it a producer?

FREEMAN It was a producer who made the assignment. I mean, at that time I was in a position where I could do more or less what I liked. I'm sure that came up in this way: "How about trying to do Jung? Do you have any feelings about that?" "Sure I'll do Jung, with pleasure, if you'll get him. If you want me to talk to him, I'll talk to him." I mean it would have been that kind of thing.

BOE Did you have subsequent contact with Jung?

FREEMAN Yes, indeed. I saw him—I forget now how long it was before he died after I got to know him.

BOE It was slightly more than two years.

FREEMAN I saw him like a couple of times a year until his death.

BOE You'd go to Zurich to visit?

FREEMAN Yes, yes.

BOE What would you do when you saw him subsequently, just talk?

FREEMAN Yes, talk and drink. You must remember about Jung—I'm sure you know this—he was a highly sociable person. I imagine he had people he liked and people he disliked, but he couldn't have been easier to get on with once one had broken the ice and been accepted into his circle. All those formidable ladies who gathered around him must have wondered what the hell I was doing there—I suppose I was seen by them as a licensed jester—but Jung and I got on well. And as a matter of fact, von Franz and Jaffé and some of the women I also found very agreeable.

BOE I've always tremendously admired von Franz.

FREEMAN I have to say, not that my opinion is worth anything, but I would say that, to the outsider, after Jung, she was the one who really stood out: apart from being obviously a woman of intellect and so on and so on, she was also a woman of great personal charm, an attractive woman in every sense of the word, very shrewd, very wise, very feminine, a very pleasing person indeed. I liked her enormously.

BOE There is this early image of Freud liking to drink and Jung being something of a teetotaler. What would you and Jung drink? Whiskey? Wine?

FREEMAN With Jung, wine. I don't remember whether he or I might have had a glass of whiskey, but he had a wine cellar which he delighted in. It wasn't actually a very distinguished one, but he took pleasure and pride in it. He enjoyed drinking wine, and he enjoyed going and fetching a special bottle and saying, "Try this."

BOE It's a pleasure many of us like. There's something about going down into the darkness of the cellar and getting the wine that is almost a Jungian symbol in itself.

FREEMAN I remember on one particular occasion at lunch where Jung disappeared certainly twice to fetch out another bottle because he wanted to try it, to share the experience and to say, "What do you think about this? A bit dry for you?" And so on.

BOE Have you kept contact with any of those other people?

FREEMAN Not really, no. For a short time, I did come back to Zurich, but . . . .

BOE Your interview with Jung was very influential on me. That's why I was so charmed to see you at Davis. You can read someone's books and then meet the person and be disappointed. It was such a relief for me to see Jung as a person, through your filmed interview, and find him charming.

FREEMAN I think I would say that, even if you hadn't been steeped in Jung all your life, you would nonetheless have been extraordinarily struck by him and taken by him, as a human being, by everything about him—his gigantic size, for instance. He was a handsome man. I don't know if handsome would be the first thing you would think of, but nonetheless he was a very handsome man. I'm not small and he towered over me even at the age of almost 80. He had great physical strength, and constantly in his conversation he made references or allusions back to his physical strength. I don't think I ever exactly discussed that with him, but he clearly did take great pride in his peasant ancestry and being stronger than the kid on the next block and so on.

BOE This seems perfectly natural to me.

FREEMAN That's right. I think one would, and I imagine that when Jung was in his prime he must have been about six foot five and hugely broad, a very striking physical specimen. Then he had this absolutely dazzling smile and bellow of laughter. He was the most unsolemn shrink that you could ever expect to meet anywhere, irreverent to the end. I suspect that with psychologists and especially with Swiss ones, sense of humor isn't the very first thing that comes to mind, but Jung was very capable of joking about himself—I mean constant jokes about the length of Jungian analysis and never escaping from it once it's got you.

BOE Are there any specific highlights of conversations that you recall?

FREEMAN I think probably not. (*pause*) The time at the end of his life he was very much—I think one might say obsessed, except that he was a balanced man, so obsession is not necessarily quite the right word to use with him—but he was very much, at any rate, preoccupied by a thought I never totally understood but you probably will: that this is the Marian age, in which the female was going to dominate and a lot of symbolism about Mary and the mother of God and so on. And how it wasn't only accidental that the Catholic church had recently become much more obsessed with Mary and so on. Well, I'm quite capable of understanding the general drift of that thinking, but I can't put it to you quite accurately, because I didn't understand it sufficiently clearly myself at the time, but he talked a lot about that. I suppose if I had to pick out one theme of conversation in those last years of his life, that perhaps would be it. I mean, a lot of the conversation was ordinary trivial conversation. You didn't have high-minded conversations all the time with Jung. But he did again and again hark back to this thought of his that we were moving into what he called the Marian age.

BOE Doesn't this "Marian age" relate to women's liberation?

FREEMAN Well, that's right. I mean it's quite clear that Jung was talking about something slightly other than women's lib, but women's lib would have fitted into it very well.

BOE As sort of a practical concomitant of this psychological change?

FREEMAN I think this is certainly part of what he was thinking of.

BOE In your interview he says that a great change in our psychological attitude is imminent. Do you think there has been such a great change in our psychological attitude in the thirty years since that time?

FREEMAN I don't know. I'd just be being pompous and pretentious if I tried to answer.

BOE I just ask because at my age, I wish there would be signs of such a change.

FREEMAN Yes. He would've been very much interested in people like Indira Gandhi and Margaret Thatcher and so on. I think he'd have been very much interested in the female of the species taking over. You see he died before Margaret Thatcher was ever heard of. Well, not before Indira Gandhi was heard of, because after all she was born practically royal—she'd been known about since she was a child—but before she came to power. He knew about Golda Meir, but I think he would have been very much interested in all that.

And then the other thing he was, of course—there's nothing new in this but I can confirm that it showed in his conversation—he was *terribly* ambivalent about Freud, to whom he clearly owed an enormous lot and whom he clearly loved in a way and up to a point, but about whom he had very considerable reservations.

BOE But when you say ambivalent, it's obvious he still respected him.

FREEMAN Oh enormously, and I think still *loved* him in a way probably. It was as if he wanted to be critical of Freud but was very much afraid that if he were critical, he would be in some way disloyal to another element in his life, which he valued and respected very much.

BOE That's sort of charming, too, I think.

FREEMAN Yes, very, very. I mean we experience this in some way or another, but not usually with people like Freud.

BOE The people most people owe a debt to but are ambivalent towards, no one has heard of.

FREEMAN Right.

BOE Since you're a political person, I assume you sometimes discussed politics.

FREEMAN I imagine so, but I honestly don't know. It's funny I don't have any clear memory of this at all. I think he was probably of the right rather than the left, but he wasn't a political person, I feel sure.

BOE That would make sense. Did meeting a man of his eminence change you or influence you in your life?

FREEMAN Well, I don't know. I could easily give you a false answer to that question. I wonder what the truthful answer is. I think that perhaps it has, in a way, but I think maybe not quite the sort of way that you mean. I think, for instance, if one is strictly truthful, it makes some slight ripple on your life to know that you have met with someone who is quite as distinguished, quite as eminent as that and found that you could deal with him man to man, that he is after all just an ordinary person. Do you see what I mean? I think even that makes some kind of impact, and certainly I did feel that about him.

Although I have never had the time (I'm not sure I even had the inclination, to be truthful about it) to dig into this area of life and follow it up, I think I also learned from him that human beings are very much more complicated than one readily assumes and that whether looking at yourself or looking at anybody else, you want to think very carefully before you assess people on the basis just of their external symptoms.

I suppose I learned something else, too, but in a way I'd come to the same conclusion by a different route, by studying the classics when young. But I suppose I did learn that the highest goal in life for any individual is completing or getting as near as you can to completing the process of individuation. I think if you asked me if I had taken anything away by way of heritage from having known him, I would think perhaps it was an abiding consciousness that while I'd made some progress toward my own individuation, I've never completed it, and with luck I will live long enough to complete it.

BOE Wonderful. How nice to hear someone here at U. C. Davis actually allude to individuation as being important.

FREEMAN I really believe that.

BOE That's such a good statement, it may be a good place to end the interview.

FREEMAN There's one question you haven't asked me, and there's no reason you should have at all, except that you've been bringing him back to me rather vividly as we talk. Well, there are two things that might just add a little bit of extra dimension.

You asked me about drinking and so on; you didn't ask me about women. Now I don't have any notion seriously about what his exact relations were with this whole group of women who surrounded him. None of my business, and to be truthful I don't think I was even particularly interested, but what you couldn't help but noticing was the enormous pleasure he took in women and in their company. Right to the end of his life. I mean, I remember dining with him in Zurich one evening and having brought a lady with me, whom he had asked me to bring with me, and he very properly sat her on his right hand side at the table, and I doubt if his hand was off her knee for the whole period of the dinner.

BOE Well, I love that.

FREEMAN Well, that's terribly zesty and gutsy. I thought that was absolutely fine. And if ever people get sort of over solemn and over spiritual about Jung, let them remember that this was a big giant of a peasant, with very high intellect, but with very, very full human instincts at the same time.

The other thing is an interesting experience I had with him. It was very, very difficult, and in some ways even painful, trying to edit his last book, *Man and His Symbols*, which he wrote for Doubleday. Doubleday asked me to act as the intermediary and persuade him to write it, which I did, and he made it a condition that I should edit it. Now this was a very unworldly thing of him to do, because in the first place I hadn't got the time. At that time I was very busy, and also, of course, I wasn't capable of doing it. I mean *you* might have been able to edit it for him, but I couldn't. I therefore had to take on the responsibility of delivering an intelligible and publishable manuscript for Doubleday without really understanding a great deal of what it was about. I had to draw a great deal on the experience of other people who did know. I mean, von Franz helped me a bit, Joe Henderson in San Francisco helped a bit, Anthony Storr in London helped a bit, and above all Norman Mackenzie, a professor at Sussex University and an old journalistic colleague—but, you know, I was completely as sea. You know, all I was trying to do was to make certain that the English was intelligible and the paragraphs were the right length.

But it's characteristic of Jung, I think, that he made my job ten times more difficult than it otherwise would have been, because he insisted on writing his part of that book in English. Now his English was very good colloquial English for speaking, but, you know, he couldn't write in English. If he'd written the bloody thing in German and gotten someone competent to translate it, one would have had something to go on, but it was written in sort of *Germanic* English, like a German spy in a B film. Having to edit that really was absolute murder. I had to turn it into English without distorting the meaning, which I didn't understand anyway! I mean I'm glad I helped to do it, because it's rather nice to have one's name associated with Jung—but it was very, very difficult.

BOE Well, the interview and that book are probably the two things that have most popularized Jung.

FREEMAN Well, that was the idea. I think I've written somewhere that the argument that moved him to write the book was that at the end of his life he felt he really ought to make one effort to reach out and talk to the people. I said that, I wonder, in the preface?

BOE Yes, I remember reading something like that.

[He gets *Man and His Symbols*, paperback version, from his bookcase, thumbing through it as he talks.]

FREEMAN He told me how after I'd been to talk to him—he'd been very unhelpful and obviously half made his mind up to say no—he'd had a dream in which he saw himself as standing on a podium in a great marketplace and addressing a multitude of people, and he woke up and said, "Yes, I'll do this book." And that's how it came to be done. I'm sure it is here (*finds page in the introduction*), oh yes: "He dreamed that instead of sitting in his study and talking to the great doctors and psychiatrists who used to call on him from all over the world, he was standing in a public place and addressing a multitude of people who were listening with rapt attention and *understanding what he said* . . . ." I don't think he made the whole thing up. I don't think he did.

BOE That's a good book to use with students, because it's so accessible.

FREEMAN Yes, it is accessible, but Jung's own section of it was the difficult one, I think entirely for reasons of vanity: he wanted to demonstrate that he could write English as well as anybody else.

BOE Who chose the illustrations for the book?

FREEMAN He chose the pictures to a great extent. I helped him choose them. I've now forgotten whether he had a final power of veto or not, but he largely chose them. He may not have chosen every last one, but he largely chose them.

BOE Any other memories?

FREEMAN The only other thing that is in my mind at all at the moment is what I couldn't help noticing when he died. I went to his funeral, and it wasn't very big. I've forgotten how many people were there, but it wasn't a great occasion at all. I remember thinking that I wouldn't mind this for my own funeral at all because, on the whole, "the great and the good" weren't there. I expect there were one or two distinguished celebrities there—I've forgotten. It was his family, and his lovers, and his close associates, and so on. It was wholly people who really cared about him. I remember thinking at the time, "Well, it's a good way to send the old boy off." Because he really was a very personal man indeed, who had close and intimate relations with these people. And here they were, all gathered to say goodbye to him. And there wasn't a general, or a prime minister, or a pope, in sight.

This seemed a good place to end the interview, and anyway I knew there were students waiting to talk to Freeman. As I left, he told me, "For God's sake, don't give me any airs that I haven't claimed, will you?"

I assured him the piece would be basically a transcript, although I might give some background information and, for example, describe his office "full of these wonderful cartoons and photos of your grandchildren."

To this Freeman responded, "Grandchildren! Hell, they're children." He pointed to a photo of his three-year-old, told me the cartoons were by his talented twelve-year-old and that he had four other children (the oldest 47).

As I left his office, I suddenly wished I'd asked him how old he was. So I went to the library, looked up *Who's Who*, and found "Freeman, Rt. Hon John, PC, MBE, British journalist, diplomatist and business man. B. Feb 19, '15." A former British ambassador to the U.S. and to India (as *Who's Who* went on to indicate), he was 73 years old, ten years younger than Jung at the time of the *Face to Face* interview. I felt a little like I imagine Freeman himself must have felt in arranging to meet Jung, "an eminent man," and finding "a very, very pleasing and agreeable old gentleman."

Reference

McGuire, William, and R. F. C. Hull, eds. *C. G. Jung Speaking: Interviews and Encounters*. Princeton, N.J.: Princeton University Press, Bollingen Series, 1977.

The Age of Pegasus

WHILE NO ONE CAN REALLY TELL just when the Age of Aquarius will be dawning, dawn it will. Because the earth has a great wobble in its spin (one big wobble approximately every 25,800 years), we have the astronomical phenomenon that determines the various ages: the precession of the equinoxes. Because of this wobble, the beginning of spring (0° Aries), which is the point at which the sun apparently crosses the equator going north, each year appears to be slightly before its position in the previous year (as seen against the background of the constellations). For example, around the time Christ was born, this spring point appeared to be in the constellation Pisces; thus the dawning of the Piscean Age.

The problem, though, is that the twelve constellations are each a neat 30° only in theory. In the sky, they sprawl (Pisces especially), and it's hard really to be sure where one begins and the other ends, where to draw the line between them. Thus various astrologers suggest different dates for the beginning of the Aquarian Age (when the sun at the beginning of spring will apparently be in the constellation Aquarius). Some claim we are already there, or almost there.

In 1958, answering questions at the Basel Psychology Club, Carl Jung made it clear that he felt the Aquarian Age was still some time in the future, saying, "We are at the end of the Pisces aeon and can certainly expect that with the transition to the new aeon of Aquarius, approximately 150–200 years from now, our direct descendants will experience all sorts of things" (1958a, p. 375). And in the same year, in *Flying Saucers*, he wrote, "We are now nearing that great change which may be expected when the spring-point enters Aquarius" (1958b, p. 311). In the last years of his life, before his death in 1961, Jung became increasingly interested in the idea of our being in

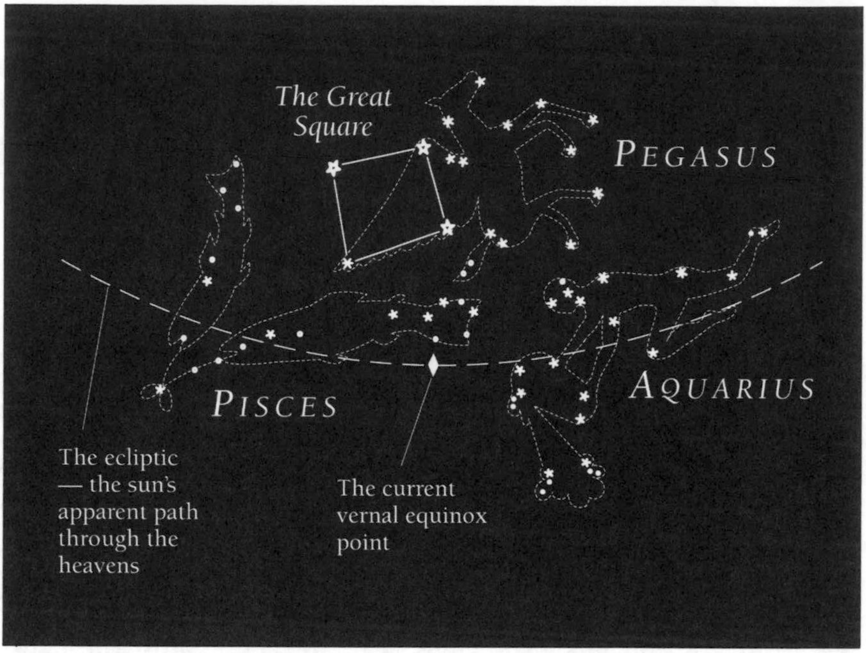

Figure 1

a transitional era between the Age of Pisces and the Age of Aquarius.

Jung's speculations about this transitional era frequently centered on the constellation Pegasus, the nonzodiacal constellation between Pisces and Aquarius (see fig. 1). Observation of the night sky will confirm that the constellation Pegasus does accompany the constellation Aquarius and does, from the point of view of the "ages," precede it. Jung thus termed Pegasus in *Answer to Job* the "paranatellon of Aquarius," that is, "what rises together with" Aquarius (1952, p. 446).

Marie-Louise von Franz writes that Peter Birkhauser once showed Jung "a new picture that he had painted of a black four-armed youth riding a grey-white boar-like horse. The rider appears out of the void. He is, so to speak, a new god of creation who promises a new spring of the spirit, riding on the white horse, the Paranatellon constellation of the Aquarian Age" (1975, p. 283). On November 2, 1960, shortly after seeing the picture, Jung wrote Birkhauser to tell him a dream:

> I want to tell you that your horse-boar-monster has had its after-effects in me! As a prelude to my latest illness I had the following dream:
>
> In an unknown place and at an unknown time, as though standing in the air, I am with a primitive chieftain who might just as well have lived 50,000 years ago. We both know that at last *the* great event has occurred: the primeval boar, a gigantic mythological beast, has finally been hunted down and killed. It has been skinned, its head cut off, the body is divided lengthwise like a slaughtered pig, the two halves only just hanging together at the neck.
>
> We are occupied with the task of bringing the huge mass of meat to our tribe. The task is difficult. Once the meat fell into a roaring torrent that swept it into the sea. We had to fetch it back again. Finally we reach our tribe.
>
> The camp, or settlement, is laid out in a rectangle, either in the middle of a primeval forest or on an island in the sea. A great ritual feast is going to be celebrated.
>
> The background of this dream is follows: At the beginning of our Kalpa (cosmic age) Vishnu created the new world in the form of a beautiful maiden lying on the waters. But the great serpent succeeded in dragging the new creation down into the sea, from which Vishnu retrieved it, diving down in the shape of a boar. (A parallel to this dream is the Cabbalistic idea that at the end of days Yahweh will slay the Leviathan and serve it up as a meal for the righteous.)
>
> At the end of this cosmic age Vishnu will change into a white horse and create a new world. This refers to Pegasus, who ushers in the Aquarian Age.
>
> I wanted to let you know of this development. (1975, pp. 606–607)

This big dream gave Jung the subject for the very last bas relief he chiseled (see fig. 2). He then commented on this carving in a letter to Ignaz Tauber:

> Many thanks for your kind suggestion that I write a commentary on my Bollingen symbols. Nobody is more

Figure 2

uncertain about their meaning than the author himself. They are their own representation of the way they came into being.

The first thing I saw in the rough stone was the figure of the worshipping woman, and behind her the silhouette of the old king sitting on his throne. As I was carving her out, the old king vanished from view. Instead I suddenly saw that the unworked surface in front of her clearly revealed the hindquarters of a horse, and a mare at that, for whose milk the primitive woman was stretching out her hands. The woman is obviously my anima in the guise of a millenia-old ancestress.

Milk, as *lac virginis*, virgin's milk, is a synonym for the *aqua doctrinae*, one of the aspects of Mercurius, who had already bedevilled the Bollingen stones in the form of the trickster.

The mare descending from above reminded me of Pegasus. Pegasus is the constellation above the second fish in Pisces; it precedes Aquarius in the precession of the

equinoxes. I have represented it in its feminine aspect, the milk taking the place of the spout of water in the sign for Aquarius. This feminine attribute indicates the unconscious nature of the milk. Evidently the milk has first to come into the hands of anima, thus charging her with special energy.

This afflux of anima energy immediately released in me the idea of a she-bear, approaching the back of the anima from the left. The bear stands for the savage energy and power of Artemis. In front of the bear's forward-striding paws I saw, adumbrated in the stone, a ball, for a ball is often given to bears to play with in the bear-pit. Obviously this ball is being brought to the worshipper as a symbol of individuation. It points to the meaning or content of the milk.

The whole thing, it seems to me, expresses coming events that are still hidden in the archetypal realm. The anima, clearly, has her mind on spiritual contents. But the bear, the emblem of Russia, sets the ball rolling.

> Hence the inscription: *Ursa movet molem. [note trs. "the she-bear moves the mass"]* (1975, pp. 615–616)

When I first read this, some years ago, I was stumped. How in the world would Russia get the ball moving in the Age of Pegasus? I could only speculate that Russia's supposedly advanced parapsychological research might eventually verify Jung's prediction. Then, with *glasnost* and *perestroika*, and with the liberation of Eastern Europe and more recently of Mother Russia herself, I could see how, geopolitically speaking, it may be Russia who gets the ball rolling.

Jung's carving and commentary emphasize the feminine—not only with the anima figure but also with the Artemis energy of the she-bear and with the rendering of Pegasus as a female, giving milk. The mythological Pegasus, as Jung no doubt knew, is traditionally rendered as a stallion, but Pegasus, especially as imaged in the constellations, is nonetheless closely connected to the feminine.

Figure 3 shows the stars of the story. Andromeda was the daughter of Cepheus and Cassiopeia. Because her mother Cassiopeia bragged that her daughter was more beautiful than the Nereids, Poseidon caused her to be chained to a rock, so that she might be devoured by a sea monster. Perseus, in some versions riding upon the winged horse Pegasus, rescued her.

Using Jung's method of amplifying the zodiacal constellations with the extra-zodiacal constellations, we can see how the chained woman (Andromeda) was the paranatellon of the Age of Pisces; indeed the constellation Pisces can be interpreted as the mythical sea monster who threatens to devour the chained woman. (Thus our whole aeon, the Age of Pisces, is imaged, accurately enough, as threatening to devour the woman, who has been kept in chains.) The myth of Andromeda, though, tells us that this chained woman is to be liberated. And in the sky the beginning of this woman's liberation can be located precisely where Andromeda and Pegasus meet (in the sky it seems to be Pegasus, not Perseus, who rescues the chained woman). The meeting of Andromeda and Pegasus (Andromeda's head and Pegasus's wing) is known as the Great Square, one of the summer sky's most easily visible star figures (an "asterism," not technically a constellation). Thus a central image of our transitional era, the Age of Pegasus, is, quite literally, woman's liberation. That this woman is attached to a winged horse suggests

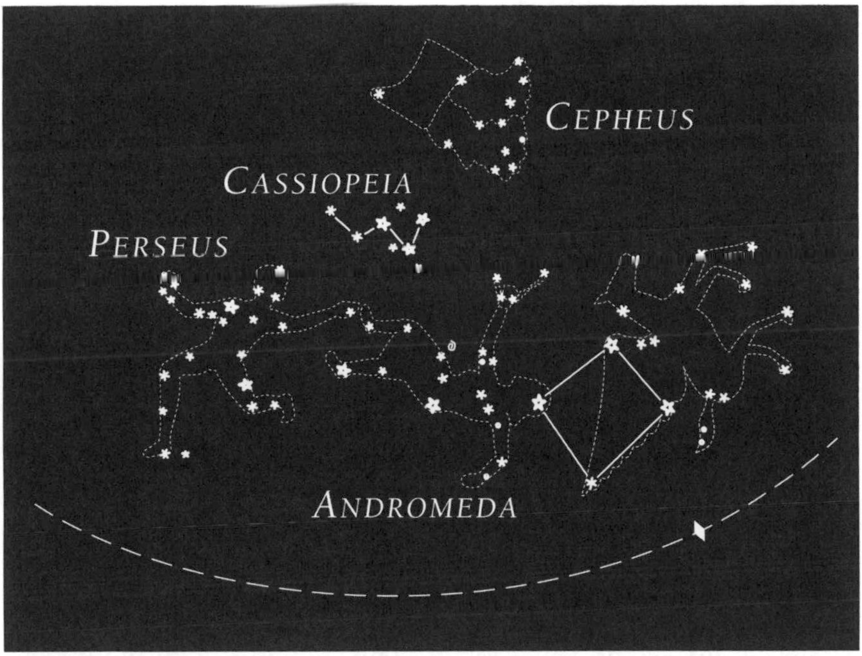

Figure 3

an elevation, a spiritualization. (A more obvious correlate of being in an age represented by a winged horse might be advances in flight, for example, space travel.)

While Jung talked about his carving from a male point of view, in terms of the spiritual energy given to the anima, the image of liberated Andromeda is even more compelling and relevant for women. This central theme of the Age of Pegasus is directly paralleled by another central idea, perhaps even an obsession, from Jung's late years, as John Freeman told me (p. 64).

The theological event which caused Jung's "obsession" with the Marian age was the doctrine of the Assumption of the Blessed Virgin Mary, the dogma of the Catholic faith promulgated in 1950. According to this dogma, Mary's soul is taken up into heaven along with her body. In the sky, as I have pointed out, the beginning of the Age of Pegasus is announced by a similar "assumption" (of Andromeda, by the winged horse Pegasus). The female principle is enskied, exalted into heaven, deified.

As Jung pointed out in *Answer to Job*, the Assumption makes possible a *heiros gamos* and forces upon our society a recognition that "the primordial divine being is both male and female" (1952, p. 462). And the sacred heavenly union, Jung went on to argue, will inevitably yield a child. In her *Notebooks*, Esther Harding summarized Jung's idea about this inevitable consequence of the Assumption: "Jung said that she has already entered into the nuptial chamber and thus, naturally, after a time there will be a child. The churchmen do not realize this, not do they consider what it will mean. They stop at the idea that there may be some sort of feminine godhead, but do not speculate on what sort of child will be born" (1958, p. 367).

Just as a child can symbolize the coming new year, so here does the child symbolize the coming new aeon. Similarly, in Virgil's *4th Eclogue*, around 40 B.C., the coming new aeon, the Age of Pisces, was represented as a divine child. Jung, in his stone carving of Pegasus and "the primitive woman," carved also the words: "Exoriatur lumen quod gestavie in alvo" (let the light that I have carried in my womb shine forth). This woman taking milk from Pegasus (an Andromeda or a Mary) is pregnant! Until her new child, the new aeon, is born, one can only speculate on what it will be like. Yeats's pessimistic speculation about our coming aeon is well known: "And what rough beast, its hour come round at last, / Slouches towards Bethlehem to be born?" While Jung occasionally hinted at some similar Armageddon—saying to the Basel Psychology Club, "This atom bomb business, for instance, is terribly characteristic of Aquarius, whose ruler is Uranos, the lord of unpredictable events" (1958a, p. 375) or quoting the Sibylline books in *Answer to Job* and his *Letters*, as saying "Aquarius inflames the savage force of Lucifer" (1952, p. 451; 1975, p. 229)—he more often saw some light in the darkness. Thus he pointed out that the constellation Aquarius pours water from a jug into the mouth of the southern fish, specifically into the star Fomalhaut, whose name means fish's mouth (see fig. 4). Von Franz quotes Jung as saying, "The sea in which the unconscious fish are swimming is now past, now the water is in the jug of Aquarius, that is, in the vessel of consciousness. We are cut off from instinct, from the unconscious. Therefore, we have to nourish instinct, or otherwise we shall dry up. That is why Aquarius is giving the fish water to drink" (1975, p. 284). Von Franz herself amplifies this interpretation: "This could mean that the task

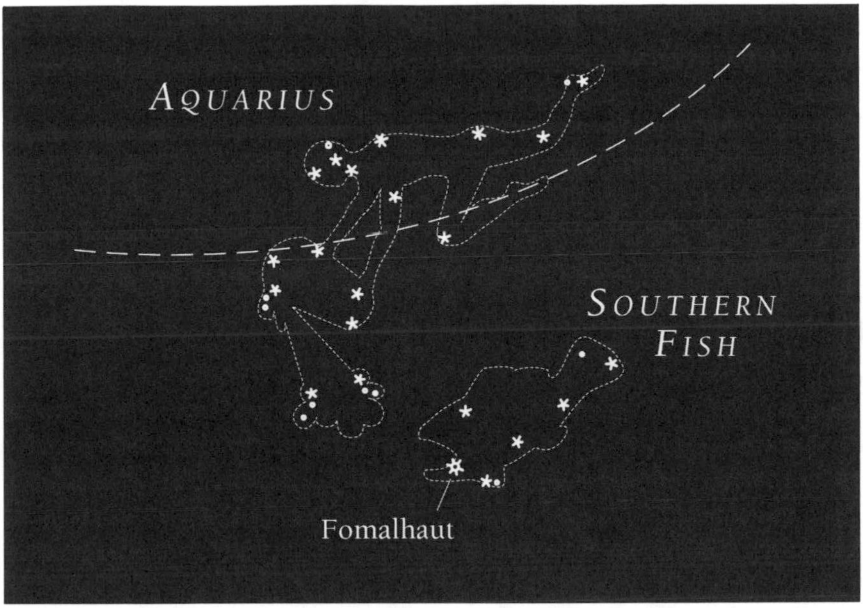

Figure 4

of man in the Aquarian Age will be . . . to give the utmost care to the unconscious and to nature, instead of exploiting it (as is the case today, for the most part)" (ibid., p. 136).

With the increasing degradation of our environment, the image of man giving the fish water needs less and less symbolic interpretation. The Endangered Species Act, for example, which mandates that we protect and recover endangered species, illustrates the increasingly active role humans are taking in attempting to nurture nature. Not everyone welcomes such control of nature as good; many would prefer to go back to the world where nature took care of herself, but in the Aquarian Age, the symbol in the skies seems to suggest, we will need to take an active role, to nurture nature consciously, to feed the fish water.

This Aquarian management of the environment would attempt to keep the wild alive through human consciousness; we would try consciously to help nature in managing resources, the wilderness, the animals, the fishes. Such scientific altruism is supposedly characteristic of the sign Aquarius, as is a certain detachment, even coldness. There is something a bit cold and detached, for example, about using computer programs to redeem nature; and there is something seemingly unnatural about managing pregnancy, about test-tube babies, etc. But if Aquarius is a bit detached, we can at least hope that this airy detachment will be brought down to earth, will be in service (in worship!) of the earth (of Gaia). And we can see this worship growing even today, in this the Age of Pegasus/the Marian age. Because in Western mythology and consciousness the female is identified with matter (as with Mother Earth), the dogma of the Assumption of Mary, as Jung told Miguel Serrano in a conversation, "is in fact an acceptance of matter; indeed it is a sanctification of matter" (1959, p. 403). Thus the sanctification of the feminine (the goddess) translates into sanctification of matter (of the earth). Thus is airy Aquarius brought down to earth.

Jung wrote in *Aion*: "If as seems probable, the aeon of the fishes is ruled by the motif of the hostile brothers, the Aquarian Age will constellate the problem of the union of the opposites" (1951, p. 87). One set of opposites we might expect Aquarius to unite is male/female. After all, Aquarius is imaged in mythology as a boy-girl (his Greek equivalent is Ganymede). Thus the Aquarian Age should bring a growth in what might be called hermaphroditic consciousness. While we might then expect an increase in homosexuality (the beautiful Ganymede seems to have been more to Jove than just his cupbearer), we might also expect a diminution of sexual stereotyping. In our current era, I think, men and women are growing more alike.

Our current era, the Age of Pegasus, should also perhaps be an age of poetry. After all, the myths say it was Pegasus who created the muses' well when, descending with Perseus, his foot struck the earth on Mt. Helicon. Pegasus's very name, which literally means "fount horse," refers to this connection with the muses' well. (It also suggests a connection with Aquarius, the water carrier/pourer.) I think that in the last decades there have been burgeoning numbers of poets: consider, for example, the astounding growth in the U.S. of graduate programs in creative writing. While there has been an increase in sheer numbers of people formally declaring themselves as poets, there is a more important change: bringing to birth in the collective psyche a more poetic consciousness.

Jung suggests that the Age of Aquarius may eventually bring to birth (in the collective psyche) a new image of God and man. Such speculation is too deep for me, but it does give me hope that the Age of Aquarius will bring the change so many of us yearn for, the change so many of the people of my generation intuited in the late 1960s. Now nearing the end of the second millennium, in this transitional era of the Age of Pegasus, we yearn for the new birth, the new aeon. As my sister, Margaret Boe Birns, wrote me some years ago in a poem for my birthday (I am an Aquarius):

Aquarius, how various
Hysterias and crises
Carry us
Aquarius
Out of muddy Pisces

References

Harding, Ester. 1958. From Esther Harding's notebooks. In *C. G. Jung Speaking: Interviews and Encounters*. Princeton, N.J.: Princeton University Press, 1977.

Jung, C. G. 1951. *Aion*. *CW*, vol. 9ii. Princeton, N.J.: Princeton University Press, 1968.

______. 1952. Answer to Job. In *CW* 11: 355–470. Princeton, N.J.: Princeton University Press, 1958.

______. 1958a. At the Basel Psychology Club. In *C. G. Jung Speaking: Interviews and Encounters*. Princeton, N.J.: Princeton University Press, 1977.

______. 1958b. Flying saucers: a modern myth of things seen in the skies. In *CW* 10:306–433. Princeton, N.J.: Princeton University Press, 1964.

______. 1975. *Letters*, vol. 2. Princeton, N.J.: Princeton University Press.

Serrano, Miguel. 1959. Talks with Miguel Serrano: 1959. In *C. G. Jung Speaking: Interviews and Encounters*. Princeton, N.J.: Princeton University Press, 1977.

von Franz, Marie-Louise. 1975. *C. G. Jung: His Myth in Our Time*. New York: G. P. Putnam.

Part II

Looking at Literature

The Wolf in Jack London

WHEN I WAS A BOY, JACK LONDON was one of my favorite writers. His adventure-filled tales were, for me, quintessential "boys' books." But rereading him as an adult and reading Andrew Sinclair's biography (*Jack*) made me realize the psychological dimension to London. He was the first person to earn a million dollars solely by writing, but he was also one of the first American writers to become fascinated by the theories of C. G. Jung. Near the end of his life, after reading *Psychology and the Unconscious*, London said to his wife, "Mate Woman, I tell you I am standing on the edge of a world so new, so wonderful that I am almost afraid to look over into it" (Sinclair 1977, p. 227).

London frequently wrote of the journey of the civilized (dog or man) into the savage world of nature. This descent can be easily understood in terms of a journey from conscious to unconscious, a descent in which the ego gets back in touch with instinct. Thus Sinclair (adopting Jung's terminology) sums up *The Call of the Wild* as the story of a dog who "transcends his role as a servant of the greed of mankind by reverting to his archetype, the wolf from which he derives" (ibid., p. 95). After the publication of *The Call of the Wild* in 1903, the archetype of the wolf became increasingly important to London. He began signing his intimate letters "Wolf," had a dog named Brown Wolf, and spent huge amounts of time and money building his famous "Wolf House." London identified with the wolf, both "the lone wolf which went about its business in solitude, and the leader of the wolf pack which survived by its coherence" (ibid., pp. 95–96). London's wolf complex manifested itself most obviously in his fascination with the violence and aggression of what he called "the abysmal brute" and in his fondness for being with a "pack" of men in a cabin in the Klondike, the forecastle of a ship, or a bar in Oakland.

Throughout his life, he was renewed by a descent into proletarian or primitive life; he was a bum, a sailor, a prospector; he was in love with boxing, with dogs, with strength.

The wolf traditionally symbolizes hunger or greed, as in "wolfing down" food. And from childhood London was ravenous for meat. One of London's strongest childhood memories (or fantasies) was of stealing meat from a little girl's lunchbox. Hunger for meat became a powerful theme in his fiction but also a destructive theme in his life. Near the end of his short life (forty years), while suffering from uremia and other disorders, London disregarded medical advice and indulged his ravenous appetite for raw meat and underdone duck. In effect, London was killed by his wolfish hunger.

This hunger and greed also manifested itself as a will to succeed. Sinclair writes: "He had quite easily achieved the fame he wanted at twenty-four . . . . He saw this incredible success in such little time as proof of his superhuman power of will" (ibid., p. 67). This iron determination to succeed is another wolf trait. Marie-Louise von Franz writes (in *Shadow and Evil in Fairy Tales*) that in order to avoid mentioning the wolf by name "it was called *Isengrimm*, which means Iron-grim, grim being the state of rage or anger which had turned into cold determination" (1974, p. 214). London wrote a thousand words almost every day of his life, working with a grim determination in the face of illness (and hangover), scandal, or lack of inspiration. Like some other great writers, London sometimes seemed unconsciously to put himself in debt, so he would be forced to write; in this way he could invoke the wolfish hunger of desperation that was the source of his will to succeed.

The wolf (in its association with war gods, with Fenris, and with the devil) belongs to the realm of the shadow, and London's most loved stories are of that shadow realm, about a masculine world of boundless energy, violence, and fear. London believed "that people respond to the literature of fear and nightmare, because fear is deep in the roots of the race. However civilized men think they are, fear remains their deepest emotion" (Sinclair 1977, p. 96). The dominance of the shadow (in London's life as well as in his literature) did have a positive side—a renewal through contact with instinct, energy, and the world of the body. And London prided himself on his energy, strength, and natural intelligence. Von Franz states that "the wolf not only carries the projection of a dark threatening animal but often of an amazing natural intelligence as well. Again, in Greek mythology, the wolf belongs to Apollo, the sun god, the principle of consciousness. The Greek word for wolf is *lykos*, which is akin to the Latin word *lux*, light (German *Licht*)" (1974, p. 214). The best of London is testimony to the vitality of the wolf, the light in the shadow.

Like other especially manly men, London's manliness may have compensated for (or helped to repress) an inner delicacy or femininity. Although he sometimes was a sexual "wolf" in his relations with women, in his literary life he often seemed overly delicate. Thus, in the opinion of many critics, an oversentimental view of love vitiated the power of many of his novels, for example, of *The Sea Wolf*. While the first half of the novel stunningly portrays a "primordial beast," Captain Wolf Larsen, the second half focuses on a romantic love story in which a weakling literary critic (who has been toughened by Wolf Larsen) must survive on a seal-inhabited island with a castaway poetess. While being marooned on a desert island with someone of the opposite sex is a commonplace sexual motif (or fantasy), London's couple remain pure, sleeping in separate quarters. London wrote in some manuscript notes a response to critics of his romantic love story:

> The critics had expected to have my hero make love with a club and drag my heroine by the hair of her head and into a tree. Because I didn't they branded my love as sentimental bosh and sheer nonsense—and yet I flatter myself that I can make love as well as the next fellow and not quite as ridiculously as the average critic. (Sinclair 1977, p. 99)

The problem though was that while Jack was explicit and naturalistic in his treatment of violence, he was sentimental in his treatment of sex. London's conscious excuse for this sentimentality was, however, economic (rather than psychological): "He did not put explicit sex into his writing because the magazines would not buy it, and he depended on his income from them" (ibid., pp. 186–187). But even though the literary standards of the era were limiting to an artist's freedom, it was primarily Jack's greed for large quantities of money that limited his writing.

Late in life, London turned his attention from socialism and political struggle to "the ways of men and women loving on this earth." He felt that the love motif was "the highest thing," the great theme, the great mystery. And he did try to write about the mysteries and problems of love. He wrote to an editor at *Cosmopolitan*, for example, about his novel *The Little Lady of the Big House*, saying, "It is all sex, from start to finish"—then adding some revealing qualifying phrases—"in which no sexual adventure is actually achieved or comes within a million miles of being achieved, and in which, nevertheless, is all the guts of sex coupled with strength" (Sinclair 1977, p. 201). In his last years, London frequently retreated to familiar patterns: he did hackwork, novelized a film serial, and wrote two undistinguished dog novels. For years he had planned to write his sexual memoirs (as a sort of sequel to his alcoholic memoirs, *John Barleycorn*); reading Freud and Jung transformed the project. Sinclair quotes from London's night pad (in 1916, the year of his death): "My Biography—The dark Abysm of Sex—rising to the glory of the Sun God. All darks and deeps and fluxes of the abysmal opening itself in God, and basing itself on hell. Write Freud and Jung, in sex terms of fiction" (p. 227). If London had lived longer, perhaps he would have joined D. H. Lawrence (whose novel, *The Rainbow*, was suppressed as obscene in 1915) in pioneering the romantic, sexual novel. Perhaps he would have written a "Freud and Jung in sex terms of fiction" book.

For much of his life, London seemed somehow to get stuck at a certain psychological stage. Perhaps he gained such energy from an identification with the shadow that he could not move on to a full realization of the anima. When his vaunted Wolf House (a mansion he was having built on his ranch in northern California) burned down in 1913, it was clearly a sign that he should move beyond his wolf phase. He did grow more introverted and less skeptical. But a large part of his soul was still fixated on the shadow, and after the house burned, he found another object for his projection of power and virility, a great Shire stallion. The stallion died on October 22, 1916, and London died a month later.

Near the end of his life, London reported a recurrent nightmare to his wife Charmian:

> It was a confession that he had long wanted to submit his own fierce ego to a darker power or to a mystery beyond his materialism. He saw in this dream an imperial figure, inexorable as destiny and yet strangely human, descending

> a cascade of staircases, while he looked up at it and waited to be vanquished. The Nemesis never reached him, but he knew he must yield to it. (Sinclair 1977, p. 228)

This Nemesis is plainly a figure for what Jung calls the Self. It's a pity London had such a difficult relationship with the Self. Perhaps because he was unable to submit his ego to a higher power, this higher power appeared in his dream as a dark and threatening Nemesis (as Death?). I think it was because his ego-shadow alliance (or complex) was so powerful that he couldn't give up to the Self, fully open up to the unconscious. But, of course, he did try; he did start (in his last years) to focus on love and sex and on fantasy and spirit. Near the end of his life, he wrote love stories, science fiction stories, fantasy stories, stories with themes like the eternity of forms. (Part of this opening up, it must be admitted, was aided by the variety of drugs he took to combat the pain of his various maladies.) Still, London's ego was always fundamentally in an adversarial relationship to the Self. His wife quoted his devastating late-life self-criticism: "Poor inner self! I wonder if it will atrophy, dry up some day and blow away." Jack did easily (and happily!) forget his inner self, fall victim to complacency, to the ease of extraversion and the greed of the wolf.

Still, I am left with admiration for Jack London as a storyteller and as a man. I am reminded of the time I was teaching a class to a group of teachers and for some reason we started talking about Jack London. Two of the women confessed (at length) that they had lifelong crushes on him. As Sinclair points out, "Jack created the image of the heroic *macho* writer" (p. 256). Of course, we can criticize much in London and his image (just as we can criticize such literary descendants of his as Hemingway, Kerouac, and Mailer), but I still admire Jack London and his masculine, wolf's energy.

References

Sinclair, Andrew. 1977. *Jack: A Biography of Jack London*. New York: Pocket Books.

von Franz, Marie-Louise. 1974. *Shadow and Evil in Fairy Tales*. Dallas: Spring Publications.

Simenon, Apollo, and Dionysus: A Jungian Approach to Mysteries

AT NIGHT, BEFORE GOING TO BED, Carl Jung liked to read mystery stories. The great psychologist explained this habit rather simply: The stories were absorbing enough to keep him from thinking too deeply and losing sleep, yet not so fascinating that he was unable to turn them aside after a few pages. And like so many of us, he loved to read about *other* people's problems. He was especially fond of Georges Simenon's mysteries.

By considering Simenon we can gain a deeper understanding of Jung and the mystery. Simenon's first detective novel was *Maigret and the Enigmatic Lett*. It is here that he first defined his central character, Inspector Maigret. Maigret triumphs not through intellect or courage, but through a psychological understanding of the criminal, built out of sympathetic feeling and, above all, intuition. Simenon emphasizes the "kind of intimacy" that always grows up between detective and criminal, who for weeks and months concentrate almost entirely upon each other. Maigret finally solves this mystery (which involves a schizophrenic twin) by studying old photographs and finding out childhood secrets. He solves the case by looking for the human factor that shows through the criminal. In this case Maigret reminds us of a psychoanalyst searching for the childhood secrets of a schizophrenic. And when Maigret finds the key to the mystery, he doesn't bring the criminal before the law but allows him the dignity of suicide.

In *Maigret's First Case*, Maigret reveals his own childhood secret: he used to imagine a sort of combination doctor and priest who, "because he was able to live the lives of every sort of man, to put himself inside everybody's mind," is able to be a sort of "repairer of destinies." Then, later in life, Maigret is forced to abandon his medical studies and finds himself, almost by accident, becoming a policeman.

Jung (like a detective or novelist) was himself a sort of combination doctor and priest, working with others' destinies, using his capacity to put himself inside another's mind more than his superior intelligence. Thus, between patient and doctor as between detective and criminal, there can occur a *participation mystique*, an unconscious bond. Such a bond involves what Jung calls relativization of the ego: if the ego can abandon its claim to absolute power, the psyche can open up to the unconscious within and the unconscious without (in the form of other people's psyches). In *Maigret and the Hundred Gibbets*, Maigret can address the assembled suspects and not need to finish his sentences. They know what he means even when he doesn't speak: "It was as if they could hear what he was thinking." Insofar as Maigret and Jung rely upon their unconscious, upon their intuition, they act without specific theory or technique. Jung denied being a Jungian, and Maigret is almost embarrassed when younger policemen want to observe his "methods."

Like a detached analyst, Inspector Maigret doesn't judge, he only unveils. Once the detective has unmasked the guilty party, he has decidedly little interest in punishing him; this is also the case in many of the books of Dorothy L. Sayers (Freud's favorite mystery writer). While sometimes the guilty party is not formally punished, it often seems that the murderer brings punishment upon himself. In one case Maigret allows the statute of limitations to run out on a group of men, since it is plain that they have already been punished for their parts in a murder (and, just as important, they have children).

Jung was also acquainted with the psychological fact that murder can exert its own punishment. In his autobiography, *Memories, Dreams, Reflections*, he recounts an early psychiatric experience. A woman came to him for a consultation, to share an unbearable secret. She had killed her friend in order to marry the friend's husband. She got her man but shortly thereafter he died, and all of life soon turned sour for her. She was condemned to a lonely life; even dogs and horses seemed to sense her guilt. As Jung commented, the murderer had already sentenced herself, for one who commits such a crime destroys her own soul.

It is easy to understand why Jung was attracted to the psychological detective stories of Simenon, to the introverted, intuitive Inspector Maigret. But we should also consider the archetypal impulses behind the detective story, and a good place to begin is Greek mythology. Perhaps the most famous mythological detective story involves the infant Hermes's theft of Apollo's cattle. At first, Apollo is mystified; Hermes has disguised the tracks so that it looks as if a giant led something *into* the pasture. Apollo first asks an eyewitness, an old man who seems to remember seeing a small child. He then uses his godly intuition: when an eagle flies by, he divines that the thief is a son of Zeus (since eagles are the birds associated with Zeus). According to some versions, he uses operatives to find where Hermes is hidden.

Apollo looks for clues, interviews eyewitnesses, uses his intuition, and employs operatives. He is the archetypal detective. While Apollo as god of divination and prophecy does have a special relation to intuition, he is also the god of law, with a special interest in murder. It was Apollo's province to exact blood for blood; it was his rule that a murderer must be purified (through punishment). Thus, instead of personal revenge (the central event of so many tragedies), the state (representing Apollo) avenges. And thus the detective, the impersonal avenger, is Apollo's agent.

If Apollo represents the detective, it is his traditional opposite, Dionysus, who represents the murderer. While Apollo inspires wisdom and was equated by Jung (in *Psychological Types*) with introverted intuition, Dionysus inspires madness and was equated (by Jung) with extroverted sensation. To Dionysus belong the ecstasies and excesses of drunkenness and passion. And as Inspector Maigret asserts in *Maigret Stonewalled*, at the bottom of the criminal mind one always finds "some devouring passion." Dionysus in his madness committed many murders. This behavior is perhaps explained by a childhood trauma: as a child Dionysus was murdered. (This is perhaps true of mortal murderers as well; many mortal murderers no doubt underwent a similar trauma, having been metaphorically murdered in childhood.) The Titans tore the infant Dionysus to pieces, but Zeus (or Rhea) helped him to be reborn. According to Orphic myth, the Titans ate most of Dionysus before Zeus destroyed them with a thunderbolt. From their ashes rose humanity. Thus, in a central Dionysian mystery rite, the initiate tore a bull (a symbol of Dionysus) to pieces with his bare hands and ate of his flesh, reenacting (in this murder mystery) the murder and incorporation of the divinity. Dionysus is therefore the god who is murdered and the god who murders; he is the god of murderers and victims alike. We can thus understand how Dionysus was sometimes equated with Hades, Lord of the Dead.

But if the detective often uses Apollonian reason or intuition, he is also deeply involved in a Dionysian mystery. His full attention is focused upon murder and murderer. And while Inspector Maigret does withdraw into introverted spells of intuition, he usually accompanies them with the Dionysian aids of beer and wine (detectives abusing alcohol and drugs is a common theme). The central event of the mystery plot is usually a mysterious (and often passionate) murder, but the plot itself is usually reasonable, fair, and intricate. And the representative of that great and reasonable thing—the law—is often possessed by a spirit of the dead, the living image of the murdered. Thus Maigret often catches the criminal by getting to know the victim. In *Inspector Maigret and the Dead Girl*, he befuddles the murderer by telling him he would have swallowed his story if he hadn't known the dead girl. Maigret's totally pragmatic and reasonable subordinate believes the false story because "no training course teaches policemen how to put themselves in the place of a girl brought up in Nice by a half-crazy mother."

Insofar as the detective identifies with the evil murderer and his dead victim, he identifies Apollo with Dionysus. (That Apollo and Dionysus were one and the same god was a paradox of the later Orphic mysteries.) In Jungian terms we could talk about the ego assimilating the shadow side. Assimilation of the shadow results in a darkening and deepening of the whole personality; a proximity with evil can lead, paradoxically, to a moral improvement. The detective is conscious of the evil he partakes in; he doesn't gloat in his moral superiority. Carl Jung, like Inspector Maigret (and Philip Marlowe and countless other detectives) saw in the whole person both good and evil, passion and reason, Dionysus and Apollo.

References

von Franz, M.-L. "C. G. Jung's Library." *Spring* 1970.

Jung, C. G. *Memories, Dreams, Reflections*. New York: Pantheon, 1961.

To Kill Mercutio: Thoughts on Shakespeare's Psychological Development

THE EDITORS OF *The First Folio of Shakespeare* (1623), John Heminge and Henrie Condell, describe their friend, "who, as he was a happie imitator of Nature, was a most gentle expressor of it. His mind and hand went together: And what he thought, he uttered with that easinesse, that we have scarcely received from him a blot in his papers." This image of Shakespeare as the poet of Nature accords with Jung's view of Shakespeare's art as an expression of the unconscious, "unclouded by ego elements" (von Franz 1975, p. 284). But Shakespeare perhaps was not always at one with his nature, nor always so at home with the unconscious.

From the characters he created, starting with a consideration of Mercutio in *Romeo and Juliet*, we can imagine the broad issues in Shakespeare's psychological development. John Dryden, presumably recounting a theatrical tradition, provides crucial information:

> Shakespeare showed the best of his skill in his Mercutio: and he said himself, that he was forced to kill him in the third act, to prevent being killed by him. But for my part, I cannot find he was so dangerous a person: I see nothing in him but what was so exceeding harmless, that he might have lived to the end of the play, and died in his bed, without offence to any man. (1684, p. 174)

But perhaps Mercutio was dangerous to Shakespeare, perhaps he did represent attitudes Shakespeare had to kill within himself—

including the Mercurial attributes of a quick mind and agile wit. I think of the famous description of the Bard's battles of wit with Ben Jonson, in which Shakespeare, like a quick English ship, "could turn with all tides, tack about and take advantage of all winds, by the quickness of his Wit and Invention" (Thomas Fuller in Schoenbaum 1975, p. 207). In just such a way does Mercutio dominate when a group of males engage in witty conversation. Consider the scene in which Romeo tries to talk earnestly about his premonition that they should not go to the Capulets' masque:

> *Romeo.* I dreamt a dream tonight.
> *Mercutio.* And so did I.
> *Romeo.* Well, what was yours?
> *Mercutio.* That dreamers often lie.
> *Romeo.* In bed asleep, while they do dream things true.
> *Mercutio.* O, then I see Queen Mab hath been with you.
> (I.iv.49–53)

The subsequent, long, and justly famous description of Queen Mab and dreams is beautiful but essentially frivolous. As it describes Mab as exceedingly tiny, so it reduces dreams to mere nothings. Romeo finally calls for peace. He tells Mercutio, "Thous talkst of nothing." Mercutio agrees:

> True, I talk of dreams;
> Which are the children of an idle brain,
> Begot of nothing but vain fantasy;
> Which is as thin of substance as the air,
> And more inconstant than the wind . . . (I.iv.97–100)

And so Romeo never does tell his ominous dream; he goes to the Capulets' despite the fact that his "mind misgives / Some consequence yet hanging in the stars" (I.iv.106–7).

A few days later Romeo has another dream. This time Mercutio is not present to keep him from telling his "vain fantasy":

> I dreamt my lady came and found me dead
> (Strange dream that gives a dead man leave to think!)
> And breathed such life with kisses in my lips
> That I revived and was an emperor. (V.i.6–9)

When Romeo's servant enters with news of Juliet's death, however, the despairing young lover's plan for suicide drives out thoughts of his dream. And ironically, in the tomb, when his kisses could have breathed life into the seemingly dead Juliet, Romeo resolves to die with a single "righteous" kiss (V.iii.114). His precognitive dream of Juliet reviving him from death, had he remembered and acted upon it, could have saved both their lives.

Mercutio scorns the magic of love and the magic of dreams alike. In the first scene near the Capulet orchard, when Mercutio and Benvolio enter calling for Romeo, Romeo retreats, seeking his heart and center, Juliet. Mercutio parodies the love world of Venus, Cupid, and rhymes of love and dove, and then mocks the magic of sexuality as he tries to "conjure" Romeo's appearance by invoking various parts of Romeo's old girlfriend's anatomy, including her "quivering thigh, / And the demesnes that there adjacent lie" (II.i.19–20). Benvolio says such talk would anger Romeo, but Mercutio replies:

> This cannot anger him. 'Twould anger him
> To raise a spirit in his mistress' circle
> Of some strange nature, letting it there stand
> Till she had laid it and conjured it down. (II.i.23–36)

This association of woman's circle with magic circle, and of penis with spirit, is entirely mocking. Mercutio, like Freud, is fascinated with the numinosity of sexuality but cannot open himself to its mysterious essence or its spiritual aspect. And so he falls into a series of low sexual images—"medlars," "an open et cetera," "a pop'rin pair"—that contrast sharply with the following heartfelt speech, Romeo's "Juliet is the sun."

Later, in the streets, Mercutio and Romeo have a convivial duel of wits, with triple puns and indecent references. Mercutio is overjoyed and exclaims:

> Why, is not this better now than groaning for love?
> Now art thou sociable, now art thou Romeo; now art thou
> what thou art, by art as well as by nature; For this
> driveling love is like a great natural that runs lolling up
> and down to hid his bauble in a hole. (II.iv.87–91)

In friendly but aggressive repartee on a city street, in the company of other males, Mercutio is at home. Such intelligent sociability is opposed to the private madness of love. With the civilized art of the man's man, the courtier ridicules love, that idiot who longs "to hide his bauble in a hole." For Mercutio, the numinosum of sexuality, the mystery of life, is something only to be joked about. But Mercutio dies. And the vision of the play opens up to the mysteries of love, the adolescent love of Romeo and Juliet finally reverberates with the archetypal image of the *coniunctio* achieved in death.

When Tybalt challenges Romeo to a duel, Romeo protests that he has good reason to love Tybalt (who is Juliet's cousin). Enraged, Mercutio exclaims, "O calm, dishonorable, vile submission!" (III.i.76), provokes a duel, and is killed under Romeo's arm. Romeo thereupon laments that Juliet's beauty has made him "effeminate" (III.i.116) and proceeds to the masculine heroism (the killing of Tybalt) that precipitates the tragedy. Mercutio embodies this quick masculine impulse for action, this unwillingness to submit; he tries to control situations with his swift wit, or swift sword. For Shakespeare, to kill Mercutio is to subdue that part of himself that attacked with quick and often ribald word play, the part of himself that played with language but didn't take life seriously, the part of himself that mocked the fool's dreams of love and magic. To kill Mercutio is to lower the ego's claims to power and awaken to the real mysteries of life.

In *Cymbeline*, the courtier Posthumus is made conscious of his lack of mastery and of the necessity to submit to forces beyond his own ego. Conscious of his guilt, he seeks death; but in prison Jupiter appears to him in a dream and lays a tablet upon his breast. When Posthumus awakes the tablet is still there; he reads the inscrutable prophecy it carries and comments:

> 'Tis still a dream: or else such stuff as madmen
> Tongue, and brain not: either both, or nothing,
> Or senseless speaking, or a speaking such
> As sense cannot untie. Be what it is,
> The action of my life is like it, which
> I'll keep, if but for sympathy. (V.iv.146–51)

Posthumus keeps the mysterious tablet out of an intuitive sympathy, for he understands his life as little as he understands the message on the tablet. His ignorance forces him into passivity; he is the lion's whelp (his surname is Leonatus) who can never triumph through heroic action, but rather, in the words of the prophecy, must "without seeking find, and be embraced by a piece of tender air" (V.iv.138–9). While Posthumus is unable to unravel the mystery of his dream, there is nonetheless a piece of it left behind, the tablet, as evidence of the reality of the dream experience. His religious vision cannot finally be dismissed as nothing.

Posthumus likens his life to a product of the unconscious, a dream, or such stuff as madmen talk of, or nothing. Macbeth sees his life in similar terms:

> Life's but a walking shadow, a poor player
> That struts and frets his hour upon the stage
> And then is heard no more: it is a tale
> Told by an idiot, full of sound and fury,
> Signifying nothing. (V.v.24–8)

The philosopher George Santayana believes that Macbeth's words summarize Shakespeare's philosophy, which was that life signifies nothing; thus Santayana concludes that Shakespeare lacked religion (1900, p. 163). While Shakespeare was doubtless a Christian—possibly even a Catholic—his philosophy as reflected in his plays is not religious in the sense of a system of tenets that give meaning to life; yet his "nothing" philosophy is naturally religious in its feeling, as in Lafeu's wonderful speech from *All's Well That Ends Well:*

> They say miracles are past; and we have our philosophical persons, to make modern and familiar, things supernatural and causeless. Hence it is that we make trifles of terrors, ensconcing ourselves into seeming knowledge, when we should submit ourselves to an unknown fear. (II.ii.1–6)

The worldly knowledge of witty courtiers and reductionist philosophers must finally be renounced in our submission to an unknown fear, to the mystery that is life. This attitude is what John

Keats, in a letter to his brother called negative capability—"that is when a man is capable of being in uncertainties, mysteries, doubts, without any irritable reaching after fact and reason" (1817, p. 81).

Negative capability involves what Jung calls "relativization of the ego." The ego renounces some of its claims to power and wisdom and opens to the non-ego. The non-ego, of course, is not all sweetness and light. Thus gentle Will Shakespeare (never in jail or duel) can sympathize with the evil of a murderer like Macbeth; and witty Will Shakespeare, apparently so in love with life, can show a fascination with the morbid, an apparent love of death. Thus mad Septimus, in Virginia Woolf's *Mrs. Dalloway*, can say that Shakespeare's secret message was "loathing, hatred, despair."

And Shakespeare's negative capability also allows him to be (as Woolf observes in *A Room of One's Own*) the perfect example of the androgynous mind. His most vivid examples of the androgynous mind are his boy-girls. In *As You Like It*, for example, the girl Rosalind (originally acted by a boy) impersonates the boy Ganymede, and as Ganymede he (she) pretends to be Rosalind, playing a love game in order to teach Orlando (the strong silent type) how to be a lover. Frequently in Shakespeare we find a female, like Portia in *The Merchant of Venice*, exhibiting supposedly masculine traits. Conversely, Shakespeare emphasizes the necessity for men to open themselves to the traditionally feminine. In *Julius Caesar*, for instance, Calpurnia has an ominous dream and implores Caesar, on the ides of March, to stay at home; but an aide convinces him that in the rational, masculine senate

> it were a mock
> Apt to be render'd, for some one to say
> "Break up the senate till another time,
> When Caesar's wife shall meet with better dreams."
> (II.ii.96–9)

This is Mercutio's point of view: the "feminine" influence of love and dreams is mocked.

Hamlet is an atypical hero. Instead of leaping to revenge, as Laertes does, Hamlet laments that he "must, like a whore unpack my heart with words. / And fall a-cursing, like a very drab" (III.i.614–15). Hamlet (like Shakespeare) is a feeling type. Throughout the play Hamlet considers his introverted feeling attitude to be too feminine. Since

Western society has often stereotyped the functions of feeling and intuition as feminine, such a man can have doubts about his masculinity. Hamlet is at home in introverted feeling (in soliloquy), but he must finally act in the outer world; so he disregards his own negative intuition as something that perhaps "would trouble a woman," conquers his doubts, and dies in a sword fight. Shakespeare seems to have effected a happier reconciliation of inner nature with outer necessity in his own life. While showing a natural sympathy for those lovers of "airy nothings," the lover, the lunatic, and the poet, he also functioned in the outer world as actor, playwright, and business man – he frequently went to court, for example, over small financial quibbles.

In the early play, *Romeo and Juliet*, the witty Mercutio sees dreams as nothings; in the late play, *The Tempest*, the wise Prospero sees our lives as nothings, merely dreams. When Prospero dissolves the vision of the masque (as if waking us from a dream), he addresses the confused Ferdinand:

> You do look, my son, in a mov'd sort,
> As if you were dismayed: be cheerful, sir.
> Our revels are now ended. These our actors,
> As I foretold you, were all spirits, and
> Are melted into air, into thin air;
> And, like the baseless fabric of this vision,
> The cloud-capp'd towers, the gorgeous palaces,
> The solemn temples, the great globe itself,
> yea, all which it inherit, shall dissolve,
> And, like this insubstantial pageant faded,
> Leave not a rack behind. We are such stuff
> As dreams are made on; and our little life
> Is rounded with a sleep. Sir, I am vexed;
> Bear with my weakness; my old brain is troubled:
> Be not disturbed with my infirmity. (IV.i.146–60)

This speech evokes an almost Buddhist feeling: all forms are empty, empty as dreams. If waking life is an apparition, however, the masque (when it is well staged) and Prospero's speech let us experience the beauty and power of such apparitions.

The dreams of our lives are rounded with sleep: at the end of our insignificant little lives we melt into the emptiness from which we were born. The idea that we are such stuff as dreams are made on always reminds me of a dream of Jung's:

> I had dreamed once before of the problem of the self and the ego. In that earlier dream I was on a hiking trip. I was walking along a little road through a hilly landscape; the sun was shining and I had a wide view in all directions. Then I came to a small wayside chapel. The door was ajar, and I went in. To my surprise there was no image of the Virgin on the altar, and no crucifix either, but only a wonderful flower arrangement. But then I saw that on the floor in front of the altar, facing me, sat a yogi—in lotus posture, in deep mediation. When I looked at him more closely, I realized that he had my face. I started in profound fright, and awoke with the thought: "Aha, so he is the one who is meditating me. He has a dream, and I am it." I knew that when he awakened, I would no longer be. (Jung 1961, p. 323)

Jung, like Prospero, focuses upon death to reveal the dreamlike quality of all life.

Shakespeare's vision always embraces both sides of what Buddha teaches in the *Heart Sutra*, the *Prajnaparamita-hridaya*: form is emptiness, but emptiness is form. Thus, in *The Tempest*, while the wise old man reveals the emptiness of all forms, his daughter Miranda responds with natural wonder to these forms, to this dream of life. So, too, does Caliban personify a felt response to the sensuous fullness of life and nature. Consider how he explains Ariel's music, beginning with a description of the sounds of the isle and ending with the wonders of sleep:

> Be not afeard; the isle is full of noises,
> Sounds and sweet airs, that give delight and hurt not.
> Sometimes a thousand twanging instruments
> Will hum about mine ears; and sometimes voices,
> That, if I then had wak'd after long sleep,
> Will make me sleep again: and then, in dreaming,
> The clouds methought would open, and show riches
> Ready to drop upon me; that, when I wak'd,
> I cried to dream again. (III.ii.134–41)

This speech, itself full of noises, in describing the music of the island, describes Shakespeare's poetry. To talk about poetry and music is to talk about sleep and dreams, perhaps because both experiences can be understood as journeys to the unconscious. Caliban evokes the soul's eternal desire for the life of fantasy. But since life itself is the stuff dreams are made on, Caliban's desire to hear again the rich music of the dreams can be a metaphor for the soul's eternal desire for life itself. Thus Caliban's speech is so full of the sensuous feeling of life, of sounds. All forms are empty, but emptiness, wonderfully, contains forms.

Santayana summarizes Shakespeare's non-philosophy of life:

> Those who think it wise or possible to refrain from searching for general principles, and are satisfied with the successive empirical appearance of things, without any faith in their rational continuity or completeness, may well see in Shakespeare their natural prophet. (1900, p. 168)

Santayana says the cosmos eludes Shakespeare, and it is true, as Caroline Spurgeon first demonstrated, that his imagery clusters around the natural and the domestic rather than the cosmic or political. For Shakespeare the hidden meaning in life is not to be found in religion or in cosmic connections. Thus King Lear, at first puffed up with his principles, is stripped to nothing, put in prison, and finally made able to feel life's meaning in a simple existence with his daughter:

> Come, let's away to prison:
> We two along will sing like birds i' the cage:
> When thou dost ask me blessing, I'll kneel down,
> And ask of thee forgiveness: so we'll live,
> And pray, and sing, and tell old tales, and laugh
> At gilded butterflies, and hear poor rogues
> Talk of court news; and we'll talk with them too,
> Who loses and who wins; who's in, who's out;
> And take upon's the mystery of things,
> As if we were God's spies. (V.iii.8–19)

As king, Lear's life and personal relations were meaningless; finally, in the simple nothings of life — gossip, old tales, songs, laughter, and prayers — he can seize the mystery of things, be God's spy.

Shakespeare, too, learned to discover the mystery in the simple things of life. In the *Sonnets* we can hear his youthful desires for poetic fame; but he gave up publishing poetry to concentrate on the more remunerative (if less respectable) career of player and playwright. Instead of pursuing fame or philosophy, Shakespeare concentrated on the old tales he wanted to dramatize, the characters he wanted to bring to life. And, paradoxically, in each great play the stream of words and events unfolds into a completeness, an experience of meaning that is, like life, not simply rational. As Jung exclaimed in a conversation, "Shakespeare talked with God!" (Kirsch 1973, p. 19).

References

Dryden, John. 1684. Defence of the epilogue: or, an essay on the dramatic poetry of the last age. *Essays*, vol. 1. W. P. Ker, ed. Oxford: Clarendon Press, 1926.

Keats, John. 1817. Letter to his brother. In *Shakespeare and His Critics*. New York: Schocken Books, 1963.

Jung, Carl. 1961. *Memories, Dreams, Reflections*. New York: Pantheon.

Kirsch, James. 1973. Review of *Psyche and Symbol in Shakespeare*. *Quadrant* 14:18–19.

Santayana, George. 1900. The absence of religion in Shakespeare. In *Four Centuries of Shakespearian Criticism*. New York: Avon Books, 1965.

Schoenbaum, Samuel. 1975. *William Shakespeare: A Documentary Life*. New York: Oxford University Press.

Spurgeon, Caroline. 1952. *Shakespeare's Imagery and What It Tells Us*. New York: Columbia University Press.

von Franz, Marie-Louise. 1975. *C. G. Jung: His Myth in Our Time*. New York: G. P. Putnam's Sons.

The Introvert in Shakespeare

HAMLET, JAQUES (in *As You Like It*), and Prospero (in *The Tempest*) are all three introverts who can be seen as self-representations of their creator. By looking at these characters and by considering some of the facts and myths of Shakespeare's life, we can better understand Shakespeare himself.

Goethe suggested that Hamlet represents "the effects of a great action laid upon a soul unfit for the performance of it" (1795–6, p. 426). In the same vein, Coleridge talked about Hamlet's "aversion to action, which prevails among such as have a world in themselves" (Coleridge 1811–12, p. 432). More recently, James Kirsch described Hamlet as torn between his true nature as a "man of spirit" and his role as a "man of the world," a role imposed on him by the ghost (his father complex) (1966, p. 48). Hamlet suffers from the archetypal tension between introversion and extraversion; he is the introvert who is forced to act in the world.

"The reflective nature of the introvert," Jung writes, "causes him always to think and consider before acting. This naturally makes him slow to act. His shyness and distrust of things induces hesitation, and he always has difficulty adapting to the external world" (1943, p. 54). This describes Hamlet, obsessed with his own "craven scruple / Of thinking too precisely on th' event" (IV.iv.41–42). Hamlet, like all introverts, knows how introspection can make one feel like a coward:

> And thus the native hue of resolution
> Is sicklied o'er with the pale cast of thought,
> And enterprises of great pitch and moment
> With this regard their currents turn awry
> And lose the name of action. (III.i.85–89)

Only occasionally does Hamlet acknowledge the value of introversion and the potential danger of extraversion. There is, for example, the bedroom scene where Hamlet plunges his sword through the arras and kills Polonius. He castigates the dead body of this rash and foolish plotter: "Thou find'st to be too busy is some danger" (III.iv.34). This is the wisdom of the introvert.

In general, though, Hamlet bemoans his own nature. When he sees an actor wail over an imaginary Hecuba, he labels himself, in comparison, as one who peeks "like John-a-dreams, unpregnant of my cause / And can say nothing" (II.ii.568–569). Hamlet claims to be a dreamer who says nothing, but of course he talks throughout the play. Much of this talk, however, is in soliloquy, where the inner stream of consciousness is shared with the audience. Even in conversation, Hamlet is often introspective, making puns and references that reflect his inner state, and remarks that the other characters do not fully understand. It is important to remember however that the term *introverted* is not necessarily a synonym for silent, nor is *extraverted* a synonym for talkative, although they are often used this way in common speech. If the attitude is inward, a rush of words can be introverted; if the attitude is outward, even silence can be extraverted.

Throughout the play Hamlet's inner-directedness is stressed. We are told how "there's something in his soul / O'er which his melancholy sits in brood" (III.i.167–168). We are told that he routinely walks for four hours at a time; that he is a scholar, a reader, and a writer; that he is certainly not "splenitive and rash" (V.i.262). Furthermore, he is possessed by an inner vision, haunted by the ghost of his father. At first the vision is seen by others, as if to establish its objective reality; later, in the bedroom scene with his mother, Hamlet alone sees the ghost. She thinks him truly mad to stare "on vacancy / And with the incorporal air . . . hold discourse" (III.iv.121–122).

While the inner vision possesses him, the outer reality confounds him. How different "fiery" Laertes is! When his father, Polonius, is murdered, he quickly returns from France, raises a rebellious mob, and assaults the palace. How easy it would be for Hamlet, beloved of the people, to raise a similar rebellion, to oust the murderer of the rightful king with a coup. But Hamlet never considers such a politically sophisticated and ambitious act. Instead he soliloquizes, meditates, waits.

Laertes, a pure extravert, has no inner questions, no moral doubts. Jung describes such an extravert: "New, unknown situations fascinate him. In order to make closer acquaintance with the unknown he will jump into it with both feet" (1943, p. 54). At one point Laertes actually jumps into Ophelia's grave! Hamlet, peeking at the funeral from a convenient hiding place, is then prompted to proclaim his grief with similar dramatic action; copying the extravert, Hamlet too leaps into the open grave.

While Hamlet meditates in solitude, Laertes and King Claudius plot together. Claudius is a particularly efficient extravert, devising plots and policies with "quick determination" (III.i.171), urging immediate action and avoidance of "abatements and delays" (IV.vii.121). Laertes and clever Claudius devise the stratagem of the duelling contest, with the envenomed sword tip and poisoned drink. Thus, it is the competent extraverts who set up the action in the outer world and who finally force the introvert—Hamlet—to act. Mortally wounded and having just seen his mother die, Hamlet is urged to action by Laertes' dying words—"the king's to blame" (V.ii.323). With weapons and opportunity provided by Claudius himself, Hamlet finally acts.

The gravedigger reveals that Hamlet was born on the very day his father defeated Norway's King Fortinbras in combat, thus winning various lands. Certainly, this heroic Hamlet Sr. represents an ideal difficult to live up to, especially for an introverted scholar. When the father's ghost visits, Hamlet, in Kirch's view, is "drawn back into the father's psychology and profoundly contaminated with the late King's spirit of crime and revenge" (1966, p. 52). When Hamlet's father dies, certain aspects of the father archetype are activated. These aspects include the patriarchal principle of revenge and the equation of masculinity with worldly action.

Shakespeare, like Hamlet, was the son of an eminent and active man. His father, John Shakespeare, was a successful businessman and was at one time bailiff of Stratford, the highest elective office in the city. When Shakespeare wrote *Hamlet* (probably in 1600), his father was past 70 and soon to die (in 1601). In writing this tragedy about the intrusion of the father complex into the psyche of the son, Shakespeare was anticipating his father's imminent death. And certainly he was remembering the recent death (1596) of his own son, Hamnet.

There is a figure in *Hamlet* who represents the successful integration of positive aspects of the father psychology: this is Fortinbras (Jr.), son of the former king and nephew to the present King of Norway (as Hamlet is son of the former king and nephew to the present King of Denmark). Young Fortinbras first appears on stage in act IV, leading an army into battle over a piece of worthless land. His example fills Hamlet, then on his way to forced exile in England, with contempt for his own inactivity:

> Witness this army of such mass and charge,
> Led by a delicate and tender prince,
> Whose spirit, with divine ambition puffed,
> Makes mouths at the invisible event,
> Exposing what is mortal and unsure
> To all that fortune, death, and danger dare,
> Even for an eggshell. (IV.vi.48–54)

Fortinbras is a kind of double for Hamlet, who is also a delicate and tender prince; but he reconciles the tender son with the powerful father, the dreamer with the actor, the introvert with the extravert.

"Fortinbras," which literally means "strong arms," is like "Will Shakespeare" a powerfully masculine name for a delicate and tender man. I imagine "Gentle Will," as tradition calls him, being an introvert and a dreamer, but one who has learned how to act in the world. Most obviously, Shakespeare learned to act on the stage, but he also acted as a co-owner and leader of a prosperous company of players and, on various occasions, as a businessman.

We can find the introvert-extravert tension throughout others of Shakespeare's plays. Macbeth, for example, constantly soliloquizes and is possessed by a vision. Like Hamlet, he finds tragedy in a crude attempt to act in the world, an attempt to make outer reality conform to his inner vision (what the witches told him).

Kirsch makes a strong case for both Macbeth and Shakespeare as intuitive introverts. While I agree that Shakespeare was an introvert, I believe his primary function was feeling. As Marie-Louise von Franz suggests, when one is unsure of the primary function, it is sometimes easier to guess the inferior function (1971, p. 16). Shakespeare did have a strong intuitive side, as Kirsch demonstrates. And Shakespeare did show a differentiated sensation function in his acute handling of the realities of his economic and business life as well as in the "sensation" imagery of his plays. I agree with George Santayana that Shakespeare had no general principles, no coherent thought-out philosophy of life. So scholars to this day search in vain for evidence of his religious orientation. T. S. Eliot wondered whether Shakespeare thought anything at all and commented that "people who think Shakespeare thought are always people who are not engaged in writing poetry, but who are engaged in thinking" (1927, p. 126). Shakespeare was loathe to make up his own plots; of all his plays, only *The Tempest* has an original plot. He was more comfortable when others had structured and thought out the plot; he could then fill in the form with his own feelings, intuitions, sensations. Shakespeare evaluates more than cogitates, moves more by pun and association than by logic. Thus I believe that thinking was his inferior function and that he was an introverted feeling type.

The word *introvert* was, of course, not known to Shakespeare. His psychological term for a man like Hamlet would have been "melancholic." Klibansky, Panofsky, and Saxl, in their invaluable *Saturn and Melancholy*, trace the development of the idea of melancholy from antiquity to the Renaissance. They maintain that by the early sixteenth century "there was scarcely a man of distinction who was not either genuinely melancholic or at least considered as such by himself and others" (1964, p. 232). Because the melancholic was a widely known psychological type, it became a stock Renaissance literary figure. For some reason, the melancholic appeared with special frequency in pastorals, where the convention developed of the author representing himself as the melancholy shepherd on the fringe of the action. Thus Edmund Spenser is Colin Clout in *The Shepheardes Calendar* and Book VI of *The Faerie Queen*, and Philip Sidney is the melancholy Philisides in the *Arcadia*.

I think that Shakespeare, following the tradition of Sidney and Spenser, represented himself as the melancholy Jaques in *As You Like It*. In this regard it is relevant that there is no such character as Jaques in the novel Shakespeare used as a source. Furthermore, just as Philip Sidney punned on his own name with "Philisides," so did Shakespeare allude to his own name with "Jaques," pronounced, according to various authorities, as "Jay-kes," "Jay-Queez," or "Jakes." Jaques is Shakes(peare), the melancholic, the genius.

Jaques's speech on the seven ages of man sounds one of the themes of *As You Like It*—that there are stages of life. Shakespeare was around 35 when he wrote *As You Like It* and *Hamlet*, and Jaques, too, is at least middle aged. Rosalind and Orlando, in *As*

You Like It, typify the young, who focus on love. Jaques and Orlando contrast themselves when they say goodbye after a brief antagonistic meeting:

Jaques. I'll tarry no longer with you. Farewell, good Signior Love.
Orlando. I am glad of your departure. Adieu, good Monsieur Melancholy. (III.ii.287–290)

Orlando goes off on his courting ritual while Jaques, a former lover, traveller, and courtier, goes off to solitude. One of the play's lovely songs emphasizes this thematic contrast:

And therefore take the present time,
With a hey, and a ho, and a hey nonino,
For Love is crowned with the prime
In springtime, the only pretty ringtime. (V.iii.33–36)

Here "prime" means both the springtime of the year and (a meaning the word now rarely has) the springtime of life (young adulthood, especially the ages twenty-one to twenty-eight).

While the young fall into the madness of love, those past their prime fall into the madness of depression. Jaques epitomizes Jung's idea of psychological change at midlife. This change is often correlated with a depression, as the individual focuses more and more upon the inevitable goal of death and feels the concomitant need for a transformation of the personality. And so Jaques seeks solitude. He tells Rosalind, "Why, 'tis good to be sad and say nothing"; and she responds with the wisdom of youth, "Why then, 'tis good to be a post" (IV.i.8–9). Paradoxically, though, the melancholy Jaques talks quite a bit, sometimes with an almost manic energy. His words can at times flow out so freely because a depression represents an intrusion from the unconscious. As Jung explains, the symbols stimulated by a depression, following a sinking into it, can be "a picture of the contents and tendencies of the unconscious that were massed together in the depression" (Jung 1958, p. 82). In forcing open a door to the unconscious, depression, for Jaques, Hamlet, and countless other artists, leads to inspiration, to poetry. Thus the good Duke Senior in *As You Like It* searches for Jaques just when he's "in these sullen fits / For then he's full of matter."

The Renaissance idea of melancholy anticipated the modern idea of genius. Jaques is melancholy because he is a genius, and he cultivates his melancholy because it is a path to increased self-knowledge. When he is told that more music will make him more melancholy, he characteristically responds: "I thank it. More, I prithee, more." In music, in solitude, in conversation, Jaques cultivates melancholy because he seeks himself. His focus is consistently introverted.

Jaques is aware of the seeming contradiction in being a musical animal. He cultivates the tension between the opposites, his awareness that man can be like a god or like a beast, that beauty and ugliness, harmony and discord are part of the full music of life.

As You Like It as a whole evokes such a double view. As with classical pastorals, there are poetic images of the golden age, but the predominant imagery is of animals and eating. Thus the spiritual wisdom remains grounded in the realities of life. Similarly, a romantic image of love is maintained, but it is balanced with cynical reminders of the realities of sexuality and fidelity. This melancholic double-edged perception lends itself to humor, for perception of a painful duality can bring laughter as well as tears. Klibansky, Panofsky, and Saxl argue that this "melancholic humor" gave birth to the "sense of humor" (1964, p. 235). And so humor, born of melancholy, involves more than jokes; the laughter that comes out of suffering and self-knowledge deepens perception.

Astrologically, Saturn governs melancholy, and mythologically, Saturn governed during the golden age. Ficino especially stressed Saturn's contradictory nature as a god who both inflicts and relieves suffering. He advised melancholics suffering under Saturn to be saved by "turning voluntarily towards that very same Saturn" (ibid., p. 271). The Renaissance Neoplatonists believed that the madness of melancholy, like the madness of love, could be a door to higher wisdom. Thus Ficino, like Jung, saw the cure for depression to be, not flight, but suffering.

In *As You Like It*, Rosalind, disguised as the boy Ganymede, promises to cure Orlando, her would-be lover, of his love madness by pretending to be his beloved Rosalind (which, of course, she really is) and playing a love game with him, letting him get his fill of love and courtship. Rosalind-Ganymede professes to have had previous success with such therapy, having driven a suitor "from his mad humor of love to a living humor of madness, which was, to forswear the full stream of the world and live in a nook merely monastic" (III.ii.418–421). First the full stream of life and love, then solitude and introversion.

It is to such a nook monastic that Jaques is heading at the end of the play. Jaques hears how the wicked Duke Frederick came to Arden to arrest the pastoral sojourners and "meeting with an old religious man / . . . was converted / Both from his enterprise and from the world" (V.iv.160–162). After hearing this, Jaques wants to join Duke Frederick, rather than return to court with the rest of the forest dwellers. And so he declares: "To him will I. Out of these convertites / There is much matter to be heard and learned" (V.iv.184–185). Finally, Jaques's melancholy has led him to begin a religious quest. His humorous scorn of society and his self-conscious eccentricity were really just ways to bring him in touch with his own self, with his own religious destiny.

Who is this old religious man so conveniently appearing off stage in act V? Early in the play there is a spiritual old man, Adam, who gives Orlando money and urges him to flee to Arden; his last appearance on stage is in act II. Jaques has just finished elucidating the seventh and last age of man, "second childishness and mere oblivion, / Sans teeth, sans eyes, sans taste, sans everything" (II.vii.165–166), when Orlando enters, carrying the weak and starving Adam, image of the seventh age. We are never told or shown what happens to old Adam after this. I like to assume he is this old religious man who appears likes a *deus ex machina* at the end of the play. As such, he would represent the wise old man, the one who has moved to a stage—the eighth—beyond what Jaques thinks is the seventh and last stage of man.

There is an old story that Shakespeare played the role of Adam in *As You Like It*. The only other role that tradition attributes to Shakespeare is that of the ghost of Hamlet's father. In both instances, Shakespeare is identifying himself with the Spirit Father. I think the archetype of the spirit, the wise old man, was activated in Shakespeare around the beginning of the seventeenth century when he embarked upon his deepest creative phase.

At the very end of *As You Like It*, Jaques refuses to attend the wedding celebrations, saying, "To see no pastime I. What you would have / I'll stay to know at your abandoned cave" (V.iv.195–196). *As You Like It* can be dated around 1599, with Jaques representing the melancholy artist, Shakespeare, about to withdraw into the period of his greatest work. *The Tempest* can be dated around 1611 and shows Prospero as having lived in an island cave for twelve years. The figure of the spiritually introverted man withdrawing into the cave represents Shakespeare's withdrawal into the unconscious in search of the sources of art and wisdom.

The Tempest, like *As You Like It*, is a pastoral, the story of a journey from city to country, from civilization to nature. This can be understood psychologically as a journey into the unconscious. The natural world is a wonderful symbol for the unconscious; and the characters, by retreating to nature, come into contact with the unconscious.

Of course, the unconscious manifests itself differently to each individual. Shakespeare often generalizes it so that those in the prime of life retreat to nature and fall into the lunacy of love. This is the extraverted point of view: the experience with country matters leads to an actual lover. One literary critic contrasts this "pastoral of love" with the "pastoral of self," in which an older person is involved in an explicitly introverted journey (Poggioli 1957, p. 174).

Prospero in *The Tempest* exemplifies the pastoral of self. His magical powers stem from his years of introversion and study. Caliban asserts that without his books, "He's but a sot, as I am, nor hath not / One spirit to command" (III.ii.93–94). Such bookish introversion can leave one vulnerable to conspiracy, as was the case when Prospero was Duke of Milan: "being transported / And rapt in secret studies" (I.ii.76–77), he ignored political realities and was supplanted by his evil brother. One midnight, this brother put him and three-year-old Miranda to sea in a leaky boat. But good fortune brought them safely to the island where they lived for twelve years before the beginning of the play.

Prospero lived on this island with three extensions of himself: his daughter Miranda, his spirit Ariel, and his servant Caliban. Ariel, visible only to Prospero, represents the spirit within Prospero's psyche. Prospero gained control of it as a result of years of intellectual introversion followed by banishment to an island. Like many alchemists, Prospero needed a servant to deal with outer reality, to carry the logs that are needed for the fire. This servant, Caliban, is also in some sense an extension of Prospero; near the end of the play, Prospero says of him, "This thing of darkness I acknowledge mine."

While Ariel is an airy spirit, Caliban is an earthy monster. Prospero disparagingly calls him "thou earth" (I.ii.314) and refers to his mother's "earthy and abhorred commands" (I.ii.273). Caliban is a would-be rapist and murderer, but he also has a certain appeal. Certainly Caliban's knowledge of nature shows his earthy side in a favorable light, as this speech illustrates:

> I prithee, let me bring thee where crabs grow;
> And I with my long nails will dig the pig-nuts;
> Show thee a jay's nest, and instruct thee how
> To snare the nimble marmoset; I'll bring thee
> To clustering filberts, and sometimes I'll get thee
> Young scamels from the rock. (II.ii.167–172)

Prospero gets an opportunity for revenge when visitors (including his wicked brother) are washed ashore by the tempest. Naturally enough, this creates tension in Prospero's normally peaceful life. As Miranda remarks, "Never till this day / Saw I him with anger so distempered" (IV.i.145). Despite his years of solitude, Prospero proves an efficient actor, bringing his enemies under the power of his revenge with a swiftness and skill that would have made Hamlet envious. But in the fifth act, Ariel turns Prospero from his planned revenge. The conversion begins when Ariel tells Prospero of his enemies' sad state:

> Your charm so strongly works 'em
> That if you now beheld them, your affections
> Would become tender.
> *Pros.* Dost think so, spirit?
> *Ari.* Mine would, sir, were I human.
> *Pros.* And mine shall.
> Hast thou, which art but air, a touch, a feeling
> Of their afflictions, and shall not myself,
> One of their kind, that relish all as sharply,
> Passion as they, be kindlier mov'd than thou art?
> (V.i.17–23)

"Passion," evocative of Christ's passion, echoes all the images of suffering that occur in the play. The airy spirit has moved downwards toward earth, showing empathy with the sufferings of the flesh; thus, Prospero's "drift of purpose" is turned (V.i.29).

Near the very end of act V, after the spirit Ariel has shown compassion for human suffering, the natural man, Caliban, shows a turn towards the spiritual. He tells Prospero, "I'll be wise hereafter, / And seek for grace" (V.i.295–296). Just as the spirit moves down to earth, the earth reaches upward to embrace the spirit. The same lesson, von Franz suggests, is taught in alchemy: "The body has to be spiritualized and the spirit has to be incarnated, both things must take place" (von Franz 1980, p. 260).

And so Prospero prepares for death, with "every third thought" (V.i.311) his grave. He gives up his magical island, his book and staff, his daughter, his spirit, and his slave. I have always been bothered by Prospero's cold tone, by his willingness to lose all that he loves and his fond embrace of death, but perhaps it can be understood in terms of an insight that Jung had following a dream about his recently deceased wife:

> The objectivity which I experienced in this dream and in the visions is part of completed individuation. It signifies detachment from valuations and from what we call emotional ties. In general, emotional ties are very important to human beings. But they still contain projections, and it is essential to withdraw these projections in order to attain to oneself and to objectivity . . . . Objective cognition lies hidden behind the attractions of the emotional relationship; it seems to be the central secret. Only through objective cognition is the real *coniunctio* possible. (Jung 1961, 296–297)

Prospero has achieved such objectivity, but nonetheless he does not discourage his daughter's love as fantasy or projection. Rather, he encourages her to embrace the mysteries of life, even as he himself grows old and tired, tired finally even of the inner mysteries. His work is finished, he is ready for death. As Jung says in the last paragraph of *Memories, Dreams, Reflections*, "The archetype of the old man who has seen enough is eternally true" (1961, p. 359).

Prospero gives up his art to return to the more prosaic life of Milan. And soon after writing *The Tempest* (probably the last play he wrote without collaboration), Shakespeare returned to life in Stratford. Is it that the inner world no longer fascinated Shakespeare/

Prospero, that he had assimilated the contents of the unconscious and was no longer compelled to work through them in his art?

"We are such stuff as dreams are made on" (IV.i.155–156), Prospero says after dissolving a beautiful vision of his own creation. Life and dream, outer and inner, are aspects of the same reality. We are all actors who at death step out of the roles we have been playing:

> These our actors,
> As I foretold you, were all spirits and
> Are melted into air, into thin air;
> And like the baseless fabric of this vision,
> The cloud-capped tow'rs, the gorgeous palaces,
> The solemn temples, the great globe itself,
> Yea, all which it inherit, shall dissolve
> And like this insubstantial pageant faded,
> Leave not a rack behind. (IV.i.148–156)

The great globe itself shall dissolve; this earth, like these our bodies, will shatter and disappear, leaving not a wisp of cloud behind. There is a pun here, for Shakespeare's principal theater (where *The Tempest* no doubt played) was the Globe. It was so named to suggest the parallel between the theater and the world. The splendid irony of this pun is that about two years after the premiere of *The Tempest*, the great Globe Theater itself did dissolve in flames. In 1613, during a production of *Henry VIII* (co-written by Shakespeare), ceremonial gunfire started a fire which consumed the whole house.

Shakespeare must have appreciated this irony or synchronicity. He wrote of the great globe dissolving and the Globe dissolved. The principal shareholders in the company were asked to contribute to the rebuilding of the theater. The symbolism of the destroyed theater combined with the demand for money perhaps convinced Shakespeare that it was time to retire completely.

Prospero is Latin for "I cause to happen" or "I make fortunate." It is a fitting name for a mage or artist, for one who controls the destiny of others. But both Prospero and Shakespeare give up their identification with the Creator, with the one who causes the action. Inflation ends; identification with the Wise Old Man ceases. In the epilogue to *The Tempest*, Prospero explicitly renounces his claims to special power:

> Now all my charms are all o'erthrown,
> And what strength I have's mine own,
> Which is most faint. (Epilogue 1–3)

Instead of a unique creative genius, we have a humble supplicant:

> Now I want
> Spirits to enforce, art to enchant;
> And my ending is despair
> Unless I be relieved by prayer,
> Which pierces so that it assaults
> Mercy itself and frees all faults.
> As you from crimes would pardoned be,
> Let your indulgence set me free. (Epilogue 13–20)

The tone is so simple, the religious sentiment so conventional. Tired and old, the magician-artist turns to prayer and asks to be allowed to leave the island, to abandon his art.

Even if Shakespeare, like Prospero, had a premonition of approaching death (he wrote *The Tempest* when he was around 48 and died at 53), his years of retirement were probably quite content. He undoubtedly spent some of his time reading, tending his garden, and visiting with his family. We know from various records that he remained active in the affairs of the town. He entertained a preacher at his home in 1614 and was reimbursed by the city corporation for the cost of the wine. In the same year, he was involved in a dramatic and lengthy dispute over enclosure (the practice of combining lands into larger units, enclosed by fences). Characteristically, he remained amicable with both sides while protecting his own financial interests.

On the whole, Shakespeare's last years were uneventful. If he wrote any final poems, they have not survived. In reflecting on Shakespeare at the end of his life, I am reminded of von Franz's description of the old man going to market in the last of the ten oxherding pictures of Zen:

> He has a sweet smile, and has even forgotten his own enlightenment. There you have the completely collective man who goes to the market with his pupil and his beggar's bowl, and has even forgotten his Satori experience

> with the gods. That means he does not subjectively feel unique, but, the story adds, the cherry tree blossoms as he goes by and that is something you would not guess when an old fellow with a fat belly goes to the market with a rather insipid smile. Uniqueness springs from him as a creative act, but it isn't intentionally in his mind. He does not feel unique, he *is* unique, although subjectively the same old man would say that he is a poor old man and what do you want of him. (1980, p. 160)

Gentle Will was open to the world; he was loved for his kind manner and human qualities. If he styled himself as an introvert in some of his plays, he certainly was open to outer reality as well. Inner visions were real to him, and he made them real for us in his plays; but outer reality, the reality of life in London and Stratford, was just as real and was also used as material for the plays. I think of Eric Neumann's term *centroversion*; being centered in the self reconciles introversion with extraversion.

A Stratford vicar and physician wrote between 1661 and 1663 in his diary this account of Shakespeare's death: "Shakespeare, Drayton, and Ben Jonson had a merrie meeting and it seems drank too hard for Shakespeare died of a feavor there contracted" (Schoenbaum 1975, p. 241). We have no way of knowing if this is true or not, but it is a memorable final image. Two old poet friends come to visit, perhaps to celebrate his daughter's recent wedding, perhaps to celebrate his birthday (also his death day). And while Shakespeare was in part an introvert, wanting to withdraw into himself, he also happily embraced friends, welcomed merry meetings. I like to think that Shakespeare embraced his two old friends at the drinking party just as openly as he embraced the withdrawal of the self into death.

References

Boe, John. 1975. To kill Mercutio: Thoughts on Shakespeare's psychological development. *Quadrant* 8(2):97–105.

Coleridge, S. T. 1811–1812. On *Hamlet*. In *Four Centuries of Shakespearian Criticism*. New York: Avon Books, 1965.

Eliot, T. S. 1927. Shakespeare and the stoicism of Seneca. In *Selected Essays*. London: Faber and Faber Limited, 1932.

Goethe, Johann Wolfgang von. 1795–1796. From *Wilhelm Meister's Apprenticeship, 1795–1796*. In *Four Centuries of Shakespearian Criticism*. New York: Avon Books, 1965.

Greenlaw, Edwin. 1961. Shakespeare's pastorals. In *Pastoral and Romance*. Englewood Cliffs, N.J.: Prentice-Hall, 1969.

Jung, C. G. 1958. The transcendent function. In *CW* 8:67–91. Princeton, N.J.: Princeton University Press, 1960.

______. 1943. On the psychology of the unconscious. *CW* 7:3–121. Princeton, N.J.: Princeton University Press, 1953.

______. 1961. *Memories, Dreams, Reflections*. New York: Pantheon Books.

Kirsch, James. 1966. *Shakespeare's Royal Self*. New York: G. P. Putnam's Sons.

Klibansky, Raymond, Erwin Panofsky, and Fritz Saxl. 1964. *Saturn and Melancholy: Studies in the History of Natural Philosophy, Religion, and Art*. New York: Basic Books.

Poggioli, Renato. 1957. The oaten flute. *Harvard Library Bulletin* 11:168–178.

Santayana, George. 1900. The absence of religion in Shakespeare. In *Four Centuries of Shakespearian Criticism*. New York: Avon Books, 1965.

Schoenbaum, Samuel. 1975. *William Shakespeare: A Documentary Life*. New York: Oxford University Press.

von Franz, Marie-Louise. 1971. The inferior function. In Marie-Louise von Franz and James Hillman, *Lectures on Jung's Typology*. Irving, Texas: Spring Publications.

______. 1980. *Alchemy: An Introduction to the Symbolism and the Psychology*. Toronto: Inner City Books.

Cats and Dogs: A Theory of Literature

I WAS PREPARING LECTURES ON children's literature, maybe spending a little too much time with preadult ways of thinking, when I realized that Lewis Carroll is a cat writer and L. Frank Baum a dog writer. This means more than that Alice's pet is her cat Dinah and Dorothy's is her dog Toto (although these facts are relevant). If cats are characterized by beauty, grace (thus music), predation, independence (thus introversion), and eccentricity (thus ambiguity), then clearly *Alice in Wonderland* and *Through the Looking Glass* are cat books. They are aesthetic masterpieces, with memorable and musical poetry; they are obsessed with getting food (frequently fish), often while the food is still alive. Alice, an independent little girl without any real companions, remains cool as a cat when confronted with an irrational and sometimes threatening wonderland. And the Alice books are unique, one of a kind, except for the fact that there are two of them. One of Carroll's most famous characters, the mysterious Cheshire Cat, explains to Alice that, in Wonderland, "we're all mad here. I'm mad. You're mad." The cat points to one exception, but this sane exception is not found in Wonderland: "a dog's not mad." Carroll's witty nonsense books are clearly feline.

If dogs (unless abused) are characterized by sanity, by sociability (companionability and extraversion), by predictability, sincerity, obviousness (even vulgarity), and by a work ethic, then the Oz books are clearly canine. They are not aesthetic masterpieces, but even if they are occasionally a bit obvious or vulgar, they are great fun (for most children, and adults, more fun than *Alice*). They seem healthy, sane; when I was a literary consultant on a child psychiatric ward, I recommended the Oz books for some of the most disturbed children.

The world of Oz is extraverted, friendly, and optimistic (even naive), so Dorothy's journeys are sociable ones. She always has company: her dog Toto, the famous threesome (Tin Man, Cowardly Lion, and Scarecrow), Billina, Tik Tok, Shaggy Man, Professor Woggle Bug, Tip, Ozma, and others.

That one of these celebrated companions, the Cowardly Lion, is a cat does not negate the essential doggishness of the Oz world. In a series as large and episodic as the Oz books, there are bound to be a few cats. Indeed the inclusive nature of the dog sensibility would have it no other way. But these cats are consistently denied their essential cat natures. (In *Alice*, on the other hand, the Cheshire Cat acts essentially like a cat, appearing in a tree, not coming when called but by its own volition, being ungovernable.) Not only is Baum's lion cowardly, he behaves more like a dog (using noise to intimidate, with a bark that's worse than his bite) than like a stealthy cat. Indeed, lions are hardly representative cats at all; unlike other cats, they are doglike in their respect for the social order (the pride), and they even share their kill.

Another Oz cat that occasionally appears, the Hungry Tiger, is often ravenous and ready to pounce on and eat a baby, but his *kind* disposition always keeps him from hunting. Because in Oz creatures are not killed for food or for any other purpose, the tiger always remains hungry. Finally, in Ruth Plumly Thompson's *The Hungry Tiger of Oz* (Book 20), the tiger renounces his essential cat nature at the conclusion of the book and ends up "thanking his stars he is not a kitten." He has been cured "forever of the desire to eat a live man," for he would rather endure stomachache than heartache. Similarly, the Glass Cat (in *The Patchwork Girl of Oz*) does not eat; she refuses to catch mice (they'd look too odd inside her transparent glass body). She is catlike, however, in her vanity, loving "admiration above everything," liking to lie around in front of a mirror. She is a "saucy, inconsiderate Glass Cat, with pink brains and a hard ruby heart." In the world of Oz, she is an object of satire.

None of the Oz books are great, but all of them (even those written after Baum's fourteen) are pretty good. Baum was professional writer (in it for the money), motivated by the work ethic, but also by the desire to satisfy the demands of an appreciative public. It was to satisfy the children who loved the Oz books that he resigned himself (after trying to discontinue the series with Book 7) to continue writing an Oz book a year until his death. L. Frank Baum himself was clearly a dog: at one time a traveling salesman and a gregarious optimistic American, a would-be Horatio Alger, he wanted to please and be loved. He consciously removed the "horrible and bloodcurdling incidents" from his books and avoided appending morals: he wanting only to entertain children. Nonetheless, the Oz books have a clear, if perhaps naive, moral vision (based on the values of friendship, kindness, and openness). Dog books are essentially moral. Iris Murdoch was quoted in a letter from Jo Brans in the *New York Times Book Review* as referring to various virtuous dogs in her fiction, then asserting "unequivocally" that "dogs are very different from cats, in that they can be images of human virtue. They are like us."

The cat book, on the other hand, tends toward the amoral. Lewis Carroll, being a cleric, was no doubt extremely moral, but the ethos of *Alice* is nonsensical, not moral. His vision was not social but aesthetic; and he himself was an extremely introverted and eccentric aesthete—plainly a cat. Cat books tend more to be symbolic, even archetypal. In the subject catalogue at the library of the San Francisco Jung Institute, there are eight references for the symbolism of cats and only one for the symbolism of dogs. Cats are associated with witches and Halloween, but there are numerous other archetypal cats, including a cult of the cat (with cat goddess Bastet) in Egypt which lasted more than 2,000 years. There are also mythological dogs, but the image of the dog primarily conjures up the social world, while that of the cat elicits the symbolic (inner) world. Patricia Dale-Green wrote a book called *The Archetypal Cat*; such a book on dogs is unimaginable.

Consider the words of the most memorized poet in the English language, Mother Goose:

Hey diddle, diddle,
The cat and the fiddle,
  The cow jumped over the moon;
The little dog laughed
To see such sport,
  And the dish ran away with the spoon.

Here, as throughout Mother Goose, the cat is associated with music—usually with the fiddle. Indeed, *cat* is an old term for the fiddle, while the curious word *catgut*—which is not made of cat guts—is a term for strings. Caterwauling, however, is reminiscent of certain untalented fiddle players. Perhaps the music of the cat inspires the normally earthbound cow to seek the lunar heights (or perhaps, as a three-year-old pointed out to me, the cow jumps over the moon because cows go moo). The little dog is clearly the hook for a young reader's identification even as the cat is a hook for the person of the poet. This is obviously a cat poem—the cat is in control—while the dog, like a good listener to the poem, laughs.

That the cat makes music and the dog laughs supports equations suggested by Greek mythology: dog = comedy, cat = tragedy. Dionysus, the god of tragedy, was frequently associated with cats, usually the panther, leopard, or lynx. These specific cats were chosen, Walter Otto tells us in *Dionysus*, because they were "not only the most graceful and fascinating, but also the most savage and bloodthirsty." Bast, the Egyptian name for cat, means tearer or renderer, and Dionysus and his maenads are like cats: they are hunters who, in their madness, tear their victims into pieces. The senseless death, the dismemberment, the disturbingly natural impulse to kill, these are the stuff of cats and tragedy. Furthermore, as Nietzsche argued in his famous essay, tragedy is born from the spirit of music. Dionysus, the mad cat, kills and makes music, thus bringing us that weirdest of all genres, tragedy.

Apollo is the god of comedy because he demands obedience to law and knowledge of limits (without an order to play against, there can be no joke). Apollo was also known as Apollo Lykios, which to the Greeks meant "wolf-god." Apollo represents social order, the sanity of the creature who obeys the rules of the pack (such as the dog or, in its earlier incarnation, wolf), as opposed to the Dionysian madness of the cat.

Certain kinds of truly great writers can be both dog and cat. Shakespeare is a cat in his tragedies (think of the mad but beautiful violence of Lear and the contempt for dogs evinced there, as in most of Shakespeare's tragedies). But Shakespeare is a dog in his comedies—teaching us to laugh at people's sport and to love them, despite their faults (a comic creation such as Falstaff is pure dog).

Because cats tend to be smaller than dogs, cat books tend to be smaller than dog books (there are only two Alice books but numerous Oz books). The great tradition of the novel is a dog tradition; the novel (with its social focus) is essentially a dog genre. Think of the great Victorian novelists working like dogs to product massive book after book; no-nonsense, realistic, big novels are invariably dog. (Dogs are essentially bourgeois, so the commercial, middle-class society that produces the novel is a dog society.)

While cats can be useful (as mousers, for example), dogs have been bred and trained for a variety of tasks, sometimes even for a life of labor. So the prose-writing professional writer is usually a dog. A paradigm of the type is Jack London, who was immensely popular with children as well as with adults. In some ways he epitomizes the shadow side of the dog writer (see "The Wolf in Jack London"). London worked like a dog throughout his life and was more a professional writer than a self-conscious artist, churning out story after story and becoming the first person to earn a million dollars solely by writing. He specialized in dog stories (*The Call of the Wild* and *White Fang* being the most famous). He often reduced his vision to a dog-eat-dog point of view, but he always had a social and political (indeed socialist) focus.

Certain highly socialized eras, eras dominated by a prose point of view—such as post-modern now, such as the Victorian era, such as the 18th century, are clearly dog eras. Alexander Pope epitomized his age (an age of prose, of concern for social order) with the famous couplet he had engraved on the collar of a dog he gave King George II:

> I am his Highness' Dog at Kew;
> Pray tell me Sir, whose Dog are you?

If plain prose tends to be dog, poetry is basically cat. While there are doubtless some dog poets, e.g., Whitman and Homer, lyric poets are almost always cats (Virgil is the classic cat to Homer's dog). T. S. Eliot seemed driven to make this identification explicitly clear, late in his life, with the publication of *Old Possum's Book of Practical Cats*.

The eras of poetic vision (such as the Renaissance, the romantic era, the pre-Raphaelite era, the modern era) are dominated by cat writers. While dogs are bourgeois, cats are aristocratic: the court-

and-castle society that favors poetry is cat. The symbolic "tiger tiger burning bright in the forest of the night" epitomizes the romantic fascination with the symbolic or inner cat. The cat poet is not a professional writer but rather an artist: the romantic poets destined to die young (producing slim volumes of luminous lyric poetry), the mad poets (creating unique poems, like mad Christopher Smart's poetic meditation on his cat Jeoffry), the poets not of this world (looking out at something else with their strange cat eyes), the misunderstood, underappreciated genius poets—all are cats.

Prose writers who transform their prose into a kind of poetry aspire toward the cat. Stream of consciousness, with its inner directedness, is clearly a cat device, and Joyce, Woolf, and Proust are cats. But such judgments about some prose writers can be more difficult. For example:

Was Emily Brontë a dog or cat? With her savage symbolic vision, her poetic style, her obvious romanticism, and her extreme introversion, she doubtless had cat characteristics. But in her life she was devoted to dogs, with her faithful mastiff Keeper perhaps her closest friend: "he seemed to understand her like a human being," her first biographer was told. *Wuthering Heights* is full of dogs throughout, but the first half (the savage, tragic, beyond human, poetic, romantic half) may be cat and the second half (with Cathy offering Hareton love as moral education, a combination of reading and kisses) dog.

Nelly foretells the developing tragedy early on, seeing Edgar Linton fall into Catherine's clutches and unsuccessfully advising him to retreat to his own home:

> The soft thing looked askance through the window: he possessed the power to depart, as much as a cat possesses the power to leave a mouse half killed, or a bird half eaten. Ah I thought, there will be no saving him: he's doomed, and flies to his fate!

This curious passage starts with envisioning Linton as the cat, but finally the reader is forced to reverse Nelly's metaphor and see Catherine, the soft thing, as the cat, as the one who has captured her prey. The tragic first half of the story, full of tortured dogs, finally culminates when captive Isabella flees Heathcliff and Wuthering Heights, on her way out knocking over "Hareton, who was hanging a litter of puppies from a chair-back in the doorway." The playful sadism that characterizes the tragic first half of *Wuthering Heights* is plainly cat.

Finally, though, Brontë felt impelled to turn her story into a comedy—with the happy ending in the prospective *komos* (marriage) at the end. In the second half of *Wuthering Heights*, we can see Brontë's desire to be true to her dog nature, which was obviously in conflict with certain cat tendencies in her life and work. She was greatly influenced by Shakespeare and in her great work tried to reconcile the cat and dog sides of her nature, much as Shakespeare, in his opus, was both cat and dog. Still, as critics have frequently complained (if not with the proper terms), the cat beginning and the dog ending of *Wuthering Heights* don't quite mix.

Was Faulkner a dog or a cat? His tendency to transform prose into poetry is certainly catlike. But while the European stream of consciousness is cat, Faulkner's differs in its high level of aggression. As his nephew once said, "My Uncle Bill was very even tempered—mad all the time." Faulkner may seem like a cat, but he is best perceived as a mad dog.

Indeed many American male writers might be seen as abused dogs: they fawn and pretend to be doggy in their love and trust, but they are not L. Frank Baums (genial dogs); they are miserable and liable to turn vicious when they get old (or get the upper hand). Faulkner has the dog's social instincts, but, as with an abused dog, this natural healthy extraversion is transformed into bark and bite. There is, then, a bad dog mode (think of Jack London), the dog-eat-dog vision of war and violence (the dogs of war), the dirty dog side of no-nonsense realism. While the poetic visions of such works as *Absalom Absalom* and *The Sound and the Fury* might make them cat works, the body of Faulkner's work is dog.

Was Hemingway a dog or a cat? He might seem a no-nonsense kind of dog, but I think he was pure cat. He was clearly a cat person in his life, owning hundreds of cats (which he seemed to love more than he loved his dogs). He imported the first six-toed cats from Key West to Cuba, where such cats, still found, are referred to as "Hemingway cats." In his memoir, *A Moveable Feast*, he reveals that during a cold poor winter in Paris, he and his wife used their cat. F. Puss, to take care of their baby: "There was no need for babysitters. F. Puss was the babysitter."

His tough-guy veneer, based on a catlike fascination with hunting prey, hides a soft purring underbelly. He reveals his true cat nature in the posthumously published novel, *Islands in the Stream*, where the chapter "Cuba" is a paean to cats, with ad nauseum details of Boise ("The Man's" favorite cat), Goats, Friendless's Brother, Littless, Furhouse, Taskforce, Princessa, and Uncle Woolfie. On and on the chapter purrs, with snippets of crisp Hemingway sentences disconcertingly distinguishing Angoras from Persians, explaining attitudes towards catnip, modes of stroking and concomitant purring.

Hemingway's style is clearly poetic, full of artful rhythm and repetition. It is also an archetypally clean style, just as cats are the archetypally clean animal. The smallness, the artful precision of his vision (the short story, the short sentence) are characteristic of the cat writer—similarly cat is the Hemingway-influenced Raymond Carver. Orwell said good prose is like a windowpane, but this is really only true of the dog prose writer. Hemingway's is a cat style and so calls attention to itself; thus it is so easily parodied. The sinuous style with the elaborately artful long sentence, such as in Henry James, also calls attention to itself and is also a feline style. Hemingway is also cat in his fascination with hunting and with tragedy. *The Old Man and the Sea* is a cat's fantasy, and "The Short Happy Life of Francis Macomber" is a quintessential cat short story, even briefly taking the lion's point of view.

Was Gertrude Stein a dog or a cat? Perhaps Gertrude Stein had such problems with Hemingway because she was such a dog person. Certainly she had a poetic style and aesthetic preoccupations—seemingly cat tendencies—but her sense of humor, her optimism, and her extraversion are clearly dog. She was a dog fancier, having had four dogs in her lifetime: her favorites, Basket I and II (two white standard poodles, who have been painted and photographed by any number of famous artists), and Pepe and Byron (two chihuahuas—both gifts of artist friends). Stein, a true dog writer in productivity, could go on and on with her writing (barking). Admittedly, Stein's tendency toward nonsense is a cat characteristic. But she is finally fascinated with the surface—there is not the symbolic, archetypal content, there is neither solution nor mystery. There is the play of a very clever, very happy dog.

Are mystery writers dogs or cats? Mystery novels are generally cat (although the hardboiled detective novel may tend more to the dog, with the hero an abused dog transformed into lone wolf). An aesthetic fascination with form propels the mystery writer, and the detective story is in essence a cat-and-mouse game. The fascination is in the catching. And for the reader, too, there is the cat fixation on solving the puzzle (as Lewis Carroll made clear, the puzzle is the flip side of nonsense, and both are cat).

Whether cat writers are better than dog writers is as unanswerable a question as whether cats are better than dogs. Marie-Louise von Franz offers a useful distinction between the creatures in *The Feminine in Fairy Tales*: "The dog reacts more as we do and shows gratitude, but the cat is a princess. It behaves as though it were conferring an honor on you, giving you the privilege of serving it and giving it milk and then it rubs itself against your leg and affords you the privilege of stroking it!" The cat is something "absolutely divine," she goes on to say, and is therefore the "right compensation for people who have existential fear." We all sometimes need the divinity the cat writer brings into our lives, the archetypal lift out of the petty, the invocation of some mysterious essence, the epiphany of the god who comes. But we cannot always live in these rarified regions. Sometimes we need ordinary existence, ordinary joys and fears. Sometimes we need the prosaic orderly world, the predictable world of love and trust—the dog's, the human's, point of view.

Part III

Looking at Life Itself

On My Back

IT WAS OVER TEN YEARS AGO THAT my wife told me she was going with her friend Marilyn's dream group to consult a feminist tarot reader.

"I bet she's fat," I said; in those days I hadn't had my consciousness raised. Anyway I had recently postulated a direct relation between spirituality and bodyweight. It seemed all the psychics I had met were fat, but I wanted more empirical evidence for my theory.

My wife was happy enough just to get to go out, to leave me home with our two toddlers. The kids had fallen asleep when my wife finally returned. She entered with fire in her eyes, and the coven behind her huddled in the doorway, flushed with anticipation.

"You son of a bitch," she greeted me. As she shared the full story, the coven in the background gradually disappeared. The tarot reader (she *was* fat, I later discovered) had told her that I was going to take a job teaching English at some Oregon or Washington college, that I would have an affair with the chairman of the department's wife, and that my wife would then be drawn into an affair with the chairman. I don't remember all the sordid details. I think I've repressed them.

"How could you do this to me, to our family?" my wife demanded, on the verge of tears. But I had no explanation. I told her that it wasn't fair to blame me for something I hadn't even had the fun of doing, but this response only irritated her more. Finally I just apologized and said I hadn't or wouldn't know what I was doing, and I wouldn't do it again or at all. This assuaged her, and I had hopes of assuaging her some more, but then the kids woke up.

A few months later, I applied for a job at Oregon State University in Corvallis. The tarot reader's prediction weighed on my mind, but what the hell, the Modern Language Association Convention (the academic flesh market) was in San Francisco that year, I had recently received a Ph.D., and I was getting depressed realizing the truth of my mother's all-purpose adage: A "whatever" (in this case, a Ph.D.) and a dime will get you a cup of coffee, or, allowing for inflation, a Ph.D. and a couple dollars will get you a cappuccino.

At the Hilton with jacket and tie at nine in the morning, I was surrounded by self-satisfied English professors and self-unsatisfied would-be English professors. I didn't have an official badge—I didn't want to spend the money to join the MLA when all I was there for was one interview—so I felt a little self-conscious. The Oregon State committee didn't comment on my lack of badge, and my interview went fairly well. After forty minutes or so of pleasant intellectual chatting—the position was in children's literature, a subject I liked to talk about—the chairman of their department asked me if I had any questions. For a moment I considered asking him my real question: "What does your wife look like? Could you show me a photo? Could the rest of the committee tell me their opinions of her?" Instead, I said I had no questions and went home.

I was understandably nervous now that the interview had gone well. Hell, if they offered me the job, I'd have to accept. I must admit I was worried less at the occult forecast of academic love affairs than I was at the thought of moving to Oregon. Later that afternoon, I decided to calm my freaked-out self by playing basketball. I went over to Live Oak Park and got into a pick-up game. But soon I realized something weird about this pick-up game: I was playing basketball with English professors!

I had only recently received my Ph.D. from U. C. Berkeley, but I had cultivated a low profile, so not many faculty members knew who I was. Still, I recognized at least two of these guys. There was James Breslin, a tall, good rebounding American literature specialist. And there was the notorious Stanley Fish, even shorter and more aggressive on the basketball court than he was in the classroom. Fish was leaving Berkeley to take a plum of a job at Johns Hopkins (where he'd soon set new standards for literary critic-as-businessman). I knew him then as the guy who'd made a reputation by arguing that the reader of Milton's *Paradise Lost* sympathized with Satan because the reader was reenacting the Fall. (Later I would recognize Fish as Morris Zapp, the protagonist of David Lodge's *roman à clef* novels *Trading Places* and *Small World*.)

Fish was, like me, a basketball junkie; indeed, his faithful graduate students had given him a leather basketball as a going away present. On the Live Oak basketball court, though, Fish was neither charming nor intelligent. I grew angry at his dirty play and played harder and harder. I skyed for a rebound, extending myself far above the aggressive tenured one below me. As I grabbed the ball, I felt a pain in my back, and, like the reader of *Paradise Lost*, I fell too. I hobbled off the court.

The next morning I couldn't get out of bed. This was the first time I had ever hurt my back. Obviously, I had taken on too much—looking for a job in a place I didn't want to move to, worrying about phantom love affairs, and, most stupidly of all, playing basketball with my social betters. So now my body forced me just to lie there. After much ice, heat, aspirin, and time, I could finally walk. The pain persisted, so I went to the doctor and got x-rays. I didn't know then what I know now: doctors can't cure back pain.

The pain lingered for months and even moved to my side. My doctor finally just told me to stop bothering him. (My doctor's really good that way. Once I called him up with some symptoms. I told him I'd read that if I had such symptoms, I should call my doctor. He said, "Thank you for calling," and hung up.) Now he told me my pains were just neuralgia (referred phantom pain), that I should just play through the pain, go back on the court. This was what I wanted to hear, and although I have hurt my back on and off for years, I've never gone back to a doctor for help.

Eventually I got a teaching job at a nearby college. After a few years there, I realized that in a spare hour I could shoot baskets at the gym. What a concept: physical pleasure at work! One day, though, the basketball court was closed, preparatory to an Elvis Costello concert, I think. Feeling that I deserved some pleasure, that my overworked psyche and body needed a workout, I decided to go where few of the middle-aged have gone: into the weight room.

The muscular and healthy boys and girls were working out on various arcane machines. Playing it safe, I mounted the stationary bicycle, but that proved as boring as bowling. I was encouraged to see a middle-aged man—it turned out to be the football coach—on one of the metallic monsters. I studied his movements, and when he got off the squat thruster, I got on. I didn't know how to adjust the weight, and I'd have left before asking someone for help (I knew they'd have sneered condescendingly), so I simply squatted down under the bars, keeping the same weight as the football coach. He's a fairly small guy, so I felt I could handle it. Up I stood, took a breath and closed my eyes. Then down I squatted, exhaling. That's not too bad, I thought, picturing in my mind my new muscle-bound self. But then I opened my eyes, and another image took over.

Directly in front of me was a young woman on the thigh tightener. She had on a pink leotard, and her ankles were somehow strapped to the machine. Her eyes were shut, and she was working hard, alternately spreading and then pulling shut her legs. I was staring directly into what the middle-aged in the Middle Ages called the gates of hell.

I unconsciously followed her rhythm. I'd squat down just as she spread her legs, stand up as she closed them. I became oblivious to the weight on my shoulders. She kept her eyes shut the whole time, her face and her other exposed skin glistening with beads of sweat. We worked together in rhythm. Up I'd go against my weight and she'd close her legs; down I'd sink, and she'd open again. Pause. Ahhh. Then up again, and on, and on, and on. My back started to hurt, but I couldn't quit. I couldn't walk out on her and our aerobic relationship. The pain increased, but I was a man possessed (love conquers all). Luckily she'd already had her way with the football coach, or I might have permanently damaged my back. She put up a fast finish, upping her pace—I tried to keep up. Then she suddenly stopped: Ahhhh. Relief. After a few moments of recovery, she left the thigh tightener for some other machine. She had never even noticed me.

After she left, I'd realized I'd hurt my back again. I tried to walk without wincing too obviously. I didn't want to have to explain what had happened. I considered looking for the girl. If I was permanently injured as a result of this, perhaps I had grounds for a lawsuit. Wasn't she guilty of entrapment, or something? Or else I could sue the gym, for setting up these machines in this provocative way—it had obviously been done deliberately by some sexually obsessed male (redundant?) looking for cheap thrills.

The pain was mitigated by my amusement at my own folly. I plotted how to tell my wife I'd hurt my back. When I got home, I told her I'd hurt my back in the weight room and would she please give me a back rub? She kindly assented, but while she was rubbing my back I told her the full story. Of course, she scowled and stopped rubbing my back, but she too could see the humor; after all, she said later, what wife wouldn't like to hear about her husband's extracurricular lust bringing him pain? Some of my friends thought I was stupid to share this story with my wife, but I needed, and luckily had someone to share the joke with. If it's funny, I tell. It doesn't hurt so much when I laugh.

A week or so ago, I was too busy. I was frantically reading final exams and papers, calculating student grades. My friend Eric had arranged a three-on-three basketball game. He was frantically busy, too, so we'd just play for an hour, then go back to work. We played with a computer-whiz student, a departmental secretary, another lecturer in English, and an older (but still younger than me) graduate student/part-time teacher. I covered the six-two 200-pound graduate student/part-time teacher, Allbutt Dissertation (not his real name).

I was violating one of my fundamental rules in playing against anyone under thirty years old, but I figured I needed and deserved the workout, and that I could just keep my distance. On the first play of the game, Allbutt got the ball. He had his back turned. I was ready to let him do what he wanted, but I didn't figure on his dangerous combination of athletic ability, basketball ignorance, and characteristic Allbutt Dissertation repressed rage. He wheeled faster than I could dodge, knocking me to the floor.

"My foul," he cheerfully admitted. I stupidly got up and kept playing, but after twenty minutes my back started aching. After an hour I could hardly walk. I staggered to a pointless union meeting, then drove home to cancel out on my wedding anniversary night on the town. I spent the next days lying down, accomplishing nothing.

A few days later, when I was able to walk with minimal pain, I ran into Allbutt in the Campus Writing Center.

"Hear you hurt your back," he politely inquired. "What happened?"

"You knocked me over," I explained.

"Are you saying it's my fault?" he asked.

"No, but it was your foul."

"Well, you shouldn't be playing with younger guys anyway," he apologized.

For Allbutt, you have to understand, this really was an apology. Like many long-time graduate students in English, Allbutt has a case of terminal irony—perhaps from reading too much John Donne. Frequently the need for indirection forces him to speak in mock professorial, German, or valley boy accents. Once, a couple of years ago, I complimented a little manual he had written. "What do you mean by that?" he responded, sincerely insulted. I realized he'd never received a straight compliment during his entire career as a graduate student, so he could only assume I was being ironic.

"Oh, no man, your manual is really terrible, a piece of crap," I rejoined. He smiled and said thanks.

This time Allbutt was right; I shouldn't play ball with young guys. And as always, I'd hurt my back at a time when I was doing too much, when I was too much with the world, too extraverted. So I was suddenly forced to do nothing. For a couple of days I mostly lay in fetal position (it hurt to stretch out); when I had to move, I hobbled around using a branch my six-year-old kindly found for me. One friend said I suddenly looked wise. And hobbled over and in pain, I felt both old and wise. I had learned once again the lesson Hamlet taught Polonius after he stabbed him though the arras (ouch!): "Thou find'st to be too busy is some danger."

When I get too busy, I get even too busy to have fun. Then I'm liable to have fun for the wrong reasons, in the wrong way. I shouldn't play basketball for a break, for the conscious goal of burning off tension or to stay in shape, but simply because I love to play basketball. The playing should be an end in itself.

I don't know if you've noticed, but lately everyone's been getting older, and everyone middle aged has been getting busier. Of course, then, every other person I meet knows all about back pain. So I really don't need the names of any more chiropractors or acupuncturists. I do enjoy hearing about new treatments or about articles in new-age magazines by doctors who have hurt their backs and then taken up yoga, vegetarianism, or tai chi. And I especially enjoy it when women crawl on the floor to demonstrate recommended exercises. But I take a laissez-faire attitude towards my back—if it's broke, don't fix it. Just wait.

Papa Was a Gamblin' Man

A Gambler's Occupation

My father, for whom I am named, became a salesman during the Depression when he discovered that his brother-in-law was actually making money selling magazines door to door. "If that guy could make twenty dollars, I knew I could make forty," he'd say, telling the story. He was also attracted to the freedom the job offered. If he made a few sales, he could always knock off work and go to the track.

When I was born in 1944 in Detroit, the youngest of five, my parents still didn't have much money. When my mother was in the hospital with me, she worried because my father didn't have enough money to pay the bill. My father, in order to avoid the hospital authorities, had to sneak up the back stairs to visit. My mother was afraid they wouldn't let her keep her baby. Luckily, my dad's company, *Collier's Encyclopedia*, was holding a regional contest: whoever sold the most encyclopedias that week got a hundred dollar bonus. And so the story goes that it was only because my father sold the most encyclopedias in the region (winning the hundred dollars) that he was able to pay the hospital bill and bring me home.

For my father, as for any good salesman, the only really hard part in selling someone a set of books was getting in the door. You figured that if you got to give your whole pitch, you'd make the sale at least half the time. The salesman needed a good "door opener," a line that would get him invited into the house to finish the pitch. My father's biggest early success came when, having worked his way up to sales manager, he invented one of the all-time great door openers: "I'm taking an educational survey." The results of the survey would always amazingly show that "your family"—by virtue of children, anticipated children, whatever—"qualified for a special deal," for example, a free set of encyclopedias with only the obligation to buy the annual yearbooks (which, the customer seldom realized, cost exactly the same as a set of encyclopedias with the standard free yearbooks). The success his crew had with this door opener led to a promotion (and to one of our many moves around the country).

Having started as a door-to-door salesman and becoming, in the 1960s, president, then chairman of the board of P. F. Collier and Son, he took on a legendary quality for the men in the field. Once when I was a graduate student at UC Berkeley, a slick, well-dressed *Collier's Encyclopedia* salesman came to my door and began his pitch.

"I'm sorry," I explained, "I already have a set. You see, my father is president of the company."

The guy smirked as if he didn't believe me.

"Yes, really, my father is John Boe . . ."

The guy stopped smirking and his eyes opened wide: "Not Boe who worked his way up?"

The motivation for working his way up was, of course, money. He made, spent, and gambled lots of it. We had lots of money when I was growing up, which was nice, and we spent all of it. My father insisted on picking up every check. He also paid for the college education of any cousin who asked for it. He bought a new Cadillac every year. For a time, I was embarrassed to come to school in a new Cadillac: I'd ask my mother to let me out a block from school so the other kids wouldn't see me.

I never had an allowance. I just asked for money whenever I needed it. My father figured that if his children grew used to the daily pleasure of spending money, they would of course want to make a lot of money themselves when they grew up. He spent money with incredible freedom, and he encouraged his wife and kids to follow his example. He would say to my mother, if out of our profligacy we ran short, "Don't worry, I can always make more money." And he could. He always knew he could, if needed, just ring a doorbell and sell someone a set of encyclopedias.

A lot of his money went for gambling. A salesman working on commission necessarily is a kind of gambler, wanting to make money but never knowing if he is going to. But the good gambler also has to have a contempt for money. If you really love money, you don't risk losing it. But if you don't really love money, losing it may just be the next best thing to winning it—at least you're in the action, not just sitting there holding it. Anyway, when you've got a salesman's or a gambler's courage, if you lose your money, big deal—you can always go make some more.

My father treated money with a certain contempt not only in his spending and gambling, but also physically. He would jam money messily into various pockets, always having a lot of it, but never needing to know just how much. When he'd leave a tip at restaurant, he'd just reach into his pocket and throw a huge handful of bills and coins onto the table, leaving an excessive but undetermined sum behind.

A Gambler's Principle

Once, in the late 1940s or early 1950s, my father went to Santa Anita with three fellow *Collier's* salesmen, Cal (an amateur magician), Commie (a former Chicago Bear), and Woody (his brother-in-law). They had knocked off early, having sold a few sets of books, and they got to the track for the third race. They decided to pool their money and let my father, the best handicapper, choose the bets. They bet twenty dollars on Aladdin's Lamp at 5 to 1. It won, wire to wire, they were up a hundred dollars, and they had a drink to celebrate.

For the fourth race, my father announced they were going to let the hundred ride on Lazy Susan, at 8 to 1. "Shouldn't we save some of our winnings and just bet twenty again," Woody suggested. My father gave him a withering glance. "Go big or stay home," he announced as if that decided the matter. When Lazy Susan won, they were up nine hundred dollars. They had another drink to celebrate.

My father didn't like to bet favorites, but he really liked B.J.'s Blaze in the fifth (at 2 to 1). "Nine hundred dollars on B.J.'s Blaze," he announced. Woody just shrugged, but Cal and Commie chorused: "Go big or stay home!" B.J.'s Blaze won, and they had \$2,700.

They had more drinks and skipped the sixth race (my father thought any of five horses could win it). In the seventh, though, he really liked his pick, Running Star. "John," Woody said, "why don't we take some of the money and split it and . . ."

"Woody, my friend," my father said, "You've got to go big or stay home."

"Go big or stay home," Cal and Commie chorused, raising their drinks in a toast.

When Running Star did win (at 6 to 1), they had almost $19,000.

What was there to do but have one more round of drinks while my father studied the racing form for the feature race, the eighth? Finally he announced his decision: $19,000 on Distant Star to win.

"Distant Star is at 8 to 1 now," he announced. "That means we'll each take home $38,000 if he wins."

"John," Woody said slowly, with some pain.

Once more father repeated the day's mantra: "Go big or stay home."

"Well, John," said Woody, "In that case, I'm staying home. I'm taking my share, it's almost $5,000, and I'm going to buy a new Cadillac El Dorado convertible, one like you have, and then I'm going home."

Woody held to his course, went home and surprised his wife—she had thought he was selling encyclopedias that afternoon—with a new car. My father, Cal, and Commie went big. They put a little more than $14,000 on Distant Star (the size of the bet bringing the odds down to 6 to 1), and Distant Star ran a distant fifth.

My father told this story many times, but he never suggested even a touch of regret for his decision. He was happy Woody got a Cadillac, but, hey, Distant Star could have won. And he had, that day, formulated (and stood up for) a basic principle of his life: Go big or stay home.

A Gambler's Family

One Saturday, in the 1940s, before he began making real money, my father had a great day at the track. Driving home, he told his friend he wasn't going to tell his wife he had won a thousand dollars. He was going to keep the win a secret. Then he could have the money all to himself! His buddies thought the plan made sense and promised not to tell.

He invited them all in for a drink, and my mother welcomed them as she always did. No sooner had she given them all their drinks when my father burst out: "Margaret! I won a thousand dollars at the track!" His friends were aghast. As much as he wanted to keep the money (to play with), he wanted to share his happiness, and he wanted to show off, to brag to his wife. He had kept his secret for perhaps two minutes.

It was in L.A., when I was four or five, that we began occasionally to go as a family for a day at the races. My older brother and sister were usually off on their own (they were ten and twelve years older than I), but my sisters Margaret and Karen and I became very familiar with the track. We loved gathering the multicolored tickets off the ground (before computers began generating tickets that all looked the same, each race's ticket was a different color). And my parents would give us two dollars to bet on each race. At my mother's encouragement, we would bet to show. We'd take turns making the pick. At first, we picked the horses by their names or sometimes by their looks (my mother said grey horses never won), but I soon figured out the tote board and the idea of odds, realizing that by betting the favorite to show I stood a good chance of winning money. So while my sisters continued to bet by name, I began playing the favorite.

One afternoon we did pretty well and my father had done very badly. Out of money, he asked if he could borrow some of ours. We of course would have been willing, but my mother quickly made him realize that he simply couldn't be serious about taking (even to borrow) his own children's legitimate winnings.

When I was little, I was mystified by how my father "read" the racing form, filled as it was with numbers and symbols. I was more comfortable with my mother's folkloristic approach. She would, for example, always bet any horse whose name referred to fire. She also had three systems: the Holy Ghost, the Alphabet, and the Chinese Remainder.

Her favorite was the Holy Ghost—perhaps because she had been a Catholic until she divorced her first husband and married my father. According to the Holy Ghost, if a number won twice on any day, it was sure to win a third time. For example, if number two won the second and the seventh race, you could bet (and she always would) that number two would win the eighth or the ninth. The first two wins were the Father and the Son; that third win would be the Ghost. And the Ghost did come in an amazing amount of the time.

I liked to help her with the Alphabet system. For any given race, you start with the first letter of the name of the first horse in the program and say the alphabet, moving your finger one letter at a time as you say each letter of the alphabet. When you get to a correspondence between the letter you are saying and the first letter of the horse's name—for example, say you say "S" when you come to a horse named Silver—you bet that horse (you sometimes have to go through the horses several times until you get your pick).

Unfortunately, the details of her Chinese Remainder system died with her. All I remember is the name and fact that it involved some strange and complicated and supposedly Chinese mathematics.

In L.A., too, there were frequent weekend-long poker games at our house. They'd begin on Friday, when my father as sales manager would pay his crew. Then he'd invite the crew to his house for a poker game. He figured if they were going to lose their money, they may as well lose to each other (or, even better, to him). Our dining room table would fill up with smoking and drinking poker players (mostly men, but there would usually be a few women, including my mother). I loved to sit next to my father or mother and watch them play, figuring out their strategy, feeling a part of the action. I'd go to bed Friday night with the poker game going on, and when I'd wake up Saturday morning, the game would still be going. My mother would leave the table to make me and my sisters breakfast or lunch, and we would go out to play, but when we came back in, the game was still there. I loved it. If didn't have anything else to do, I could always watch an hour or two of the poker game, listen to the jokes, learn the games, watch those reds, blues, and whites piling up in the middle of the table, moving from player to player. I'd stack them up and count them for my father, who usually just kept his chips in a messy pile.

Over the years there were card games of all kinds, always for money: canasta (especially popular for couples), bridge, cribbage, and almost always high-stakes gin rummy. My father used to play gin with one guy, Al, who beat him regularly. My father was a good card player, so this really rankled. He finally figured out that Al, who had a great memory for cards, never shuffled very thoroughly, putting himself in a position to make some pretty good guesses as to where certain cards were in the deck. So my dad invited Al over to play some gin. As I had been instructed to do, I asked if I could watch. "Sure," Al and Dad said. So my dad got out two decks of cards. He shuffled one, dealt and played the hand. After the hand, I scooped up the cards, and shuffled them while they played a hand with the other deck. I shuffled all day long, and my dad cleaned Al's clock.

It's possible my father was not a very good father: he was away much of the time, and even when he was home, he didn't really know how to relate to children. But I did love, and relate to, his gambling. After all, the word *gamble* probably comes from the old English *gamian*, meaning "play": that my father was a gambler meant that he played, so there were card games to watch, sporting events to go to, and the father-son pleasure of TV ball games (where we rooted according to Dad's bet).

Through a lifetime of marriage, my mother became a bit of a gambler herself (she learned to read the racing form and play cards well). In the early days, though, when they didn't have much money, she didn't like the gambling, wanting a more conventional and responsible husband. She used to tell about the time she had to leave me and my sisters (toddlers at the time) in the care of my older sister Joan so she could drive from Detroit to Indianapolis to bail my father out of jail (I never did learn exactly why he had been incarcerated). When she got to the jail, she discovered he had no money with him, only a pocketful of poker chips, which he had almost convinced the guard were actually negotiable currency and could be accepted in lieu of bail money.

One morning, also in the early days, my mother told my father that she had dreamed about a racehorse named Sir Charming. My father opened the sports page and announced that, amazingly enough, there was a horse named Sir Charming running in a maiden race at the Detroit track that very day. My mother saw what was coming and made my father promise not to give up a day's work (ringing doorbells to sell *Collier's Encyclopedias*) to go betting a dream horse at the racetrack. My father assured her that he would put in a full day's work. Then, of course, he worked half a day, went to the track, bet on Sir Charming—and won! My mother was not pleased, but the much needed money appeased her anger.

Some months later, she had another dream. In the morning, she told my father she'd had another racehorse dream, but she wouldn't reveal it unless he promised (absolutely guaranteed) that he wasn't going to go to the track and bet on it. My father reminded her that he was driving out of town that very morning for a Midwest regional sales meeting. Even if he wanted to, he couldn't go to the track that day.

And so my mother confided that the horse's name was Windstorm. My father looked in the paper and to my mother's relief reported no Windstorm running that day.

And so my father drove out of town, let's say it was to Akron, Ohio. In Akron, as so often happened as part of his salemen's meetings, he ended up at a bar. And, coincidentally, this bar had a handbook in back (a small-time bookmaker's place). So my father looked at the races being run around the country and did find a Windstorm running. He put a bundle on it and Windstorm won.

My mother should have been pleased when he got home early the next morning with a bundle of money, but she swore she'd never tell him another horse dream. And she claimed she never had another one.

While my mother consciously wanted to discourage my father's gambling, her dreams showed that she unconsciously supported it. She did want him to be a hard worker, not a gamester, but her unconscious gave her these dreams that sent him to the track, dreams that picked winners.

A Gambler's Legacy

When my father died in 1977, he left my mother a nice pension and a few stocks, but no fortune. Men who had worked for him had become millionaires, but he had gone through his money, had gambled most of it away. He was really good at the horses but protested that over the years the vigorish (the percentage the track or the bookie skims off the top before distributing money back as winnings) had increased so much that even the horses had become impossible to beat. And he regularly lost his money in TV sports, betting all games that were on TV and some that weren't. Once he drove my college roommate Victor and me from our home in Ridgewood, New Jersey, to Amherst College for the start of our sophomore year. On the way, we talked football, my father asking Victor who he thought was going to win the Ohio State-Michigan game (Michigan was a three-point underdog). Victor opined that he thought Michigan would flat out win the game. My father raised his eyebrows, pulled off the turnpike, stopped at a pay phone, called his bookie, and bet $200 on Michigan (who lost by ten).

It was his money. He made it, and he enjoyed the hell out of throwing it away. He'd fly to the Super Bowl or the Kentucky Derby (the family never took vacations). He even bought some racehorses, some of whom I saw relentlessly lose at Golden Gate Fields when I was a graduate student at UC Berkeley. One time, he claimed a horse for $10,000 (for a claiming race, you pay the money before the race and then you own the horse as soon as that race is over. The old owner gets any purse for winning). His agent, who handled the transaction, mistakenly forgot to buy insurance for the horse, so when the horse stumbled and fell at the finish line, having broken its leg and having to be shot immediately, my father not only had to pay $10,000 for a dead horse, but he had to pay the cost of the horse's killing and disposal. At least he did get another story to tell.

Once he was on a train in England with the *Collier's* vice-president, Joe Chapell. They got into a card game with two strangers, and soon my father realized the strangers were con men, were working together to cheat him and Chapell. My father's response to this was to raise the stakes and buy the men a drink. He thought it was such fun to be cheated by English con men (Chapell never noticed) that he kept the game going for the whole train ride, trying to figure out every nuance of the men's system. He felt that the loss of a few hundred dollars was well worth the entertainment the crooks gave him.

Of course, the biggest gambling pleasure comes when you are on a winning streak. In 1966, I met my parents at my grandmother's ninetieth birthday party in St. Louis (my wife and I were driving from New Jersey to Berkeley). After the celebration, we went to the track with my father and some other folks. My father was hot, hitting the daily double, exactas, long shots, raising his bets with each win. He sent me to make his bets for him (what fun to be at the hundred dollar window!) and to collect his winnings. Near the end of the evening, I wised up enough to start betting the same horses he was betting, and so I won a couple hundred dollars myself. He ended up some thousands ahead, but I'm not sure exactly how much. What I remember is the feeling of magic he gave off. For a while, you just knew he could tell the future, that he was going to predict the winner of the next race.

There is something occult about gambling. What you are doing is clearly divination. You study some numbers, look at the horses, and bet some money that you can tell the future. And when you do it successfully more times than you should, you get this rush, this almost otherworldly experience that is more than just the high of making money.

One Christmas, the whole family played a board game called something like Intuition or ESP (my father was always a good Christmas father, playing games with the kids all afternoon while the turkey cooked). After playing for an hour or so, it was obvious to all of us that my father had the best intuition, that he was better than we were at looking into the future.

My father taught me, by his example, one secret of using intuition in gambling: try to be rational. Try, for example, to figure out the statistics in the racing form. Use your thinking as much as you can, because if you're an intuitive person, your intuition will come in anyway, will lead you to your pick (which you can always find rational reasons for betting on). This rationale for handicapping reminds me of one I once heard about writing in rhyme: for some poets, rhyme is an aid because it distracts the conscious mind (which has to think of rhymes) and therefore lets the unconscious come in undisturbed to do the real work of the poetry. Similarly, the rational gambler occupies his mind enough with rationality so that his intuition can function undisturbed.

My father was intuitive, but he was also lucky. It had to have been luck when in 1965 he won a brand new Cadillac Eldorado convertible in a church raffle. Since he already had one, he told my mother he was going to give it to me for a wedding present. My mother assured him I wouldn't want such a showy car, but I was no longer embarrassed by money, so I said thank you and drove out to graduate school in a new Cadillac (which my wife drove to her job as a sixth grade teacher in Newark, California).

While I gamble only a little, I feel that in gambling I am aware of my father's legacy. So I study the form before going to the track, trying to figure it all out. I have a little legacy from my mother here, too, for once I did have a dream of a racetrack winner. It was just after graduate school, and I was marginally or not at all employed, so I spent a lot of time at the track. The races must have been on my mind a lot, because one night I had a dream of the daily double winner. The first was won by a horse named Zabu, but I couldn't quite remember the second winner's name. I only remembered that it had something to do with sleeping or bathing.

I checked out who was running every day and sure enough, within a couple of weeks, there was a Zabu (a horse new to California) listed for the first race. I went to the bank and took out some money (telling my dream to the tellers, who gave me some of their money to bet for them). I put twenty dollars Zabu to win at 20 to 1. Then I looked at the second race. For some reason, I associated Sweet Jo Mama with sleeping and bathing (my sister Joan used to take care of me a lot when I was a baby, when, for example, my parents were at the races). So I bet fifty dollars worth of daily doubles: Zabu and Sweet Jo Mama. Zabu won the first race, giving me four hundred dollars, but the second race was won by At Your Leisure. Of course! Sleeping and bathing is being at your leisure! Why hadn't I seen that? I would have won $5,000. Still, my dream did bring me four hundred.

Like my mother, I never had another racetrack winner dream, but when I know I'm going to the races, I always make sure I have my little dream pad next to my bed. The experience of having a dream tell the future, predict a racetrack winner, didn't make me an inveterate gambler; it instead made me an inveterate follower of my dreams. If my dreams can predict a horse race, then they ought to be able to tell me something about my own life.

From my gambler father most of all I received *lore*. I take my wife and daughter to the track and give them what is now my lore. My wife regularly bets the Ghost (and wins a lot of the time). We can't afford to give my ten-year-old Lily two dollars for each race, so we book her bets ourselves, at 20 cents a bet. I'm happy to say she follows Boe family principles (go big or stay home) and bets to win, not show.

Like my father, I try to stay away from favorites (if you hit two 8 to 1 shots in a day at the races, you'll win for the day). And like my father, I have a certain contempt for money, which makes gambling easy for me. It really is only money. When I gamble my father is with me, I am my father, I am John Boe. So I am pretty good at it. I do win a lot of the time. I've done well at table stakes poker (those years of watching the adults play helped), but I like the track best of all. I don't bet TV sports, mostly because I don't have a bookie. Actually, my father used to tease me about the fact that I, an academic, a Berkeley hippie, a whatever it was I was, no doubt couldn't find a bookie if I wanted one. He offered to bet me I couldn't get a bet down in Berkeley, and I wanted to take the bet, but I knew I'd lose. My world is not the world of bookies. This is probably for the best.

A couple summers ago, driving home from a Wyoming backpacking trip with three of my friends, we stopped at Reno. I decided to play roulette, having fallen in love with the game after reading Dostoyevski's *The Gambler*. My friends didn't want to play, so they hovered around the table watching. We must have looked pretty funky, having just come out of the mountains, and security seemed to take a special interest in us.

I decided to play number 17 because my father's lucky number was 17. Once at a race track in Japan, he bet nothing but 1 and 7, any combinations that suggested 17, since he couldn't read their racing form, and he won all day. I figured I might have inherited his lucky number, so at the roulette table I put a dollar on 17, and it came up. I was thirty-five dollars up. I put another dollar on 17, and it came up again! Now I was seventy dollars up, and the croupier proceeded to spin the wheel as I bet 17 one more time. This time, though, he "accidentally" threw the ball onto the ground. Security guards scurried over to pick up the ball the check out the scene. My momentary magic spell was broken by a required change of balls, so I soon quit. I was up a few dollars, but I knew I had blown it. I still think back on the chance that was given me (like the chance give me by the daily double dream). After I had won the first time, I should have let the whole thirty-five dollars ride on number 17 one more time. After all, you've go to go big or stay home.

A Time to Be Born

THE OTHER DAY I WENT OUT IN my backyard and discovered that my fruit trees had come back to life. A quince and one plum were flowering, the other plums had green leaves coming out from the buds, and even the pears and apples had buds that were obviously alive. I shouldn't have been surprised, but I was. I felt like one of the kids I used to confuse at my daughter's old nursery school: there was this huge redwood tree in the middle of the play yard, and I'd occasionally confront one of the kids, point at the tree, and say, ominously, "You know, it's alive."

I got these fruit trees, and the house that goes with them, just after last year's Super Bowl. I wanted a house big enough for my family, not one we could afford (that was clearly impossible), but one we could qualify to get a loan on. The big yard was just a bonus. Still, I had regretted the fact that it had all these dead trees in it, and I was resolved to cut away all this dead wood and plant myself some fruit trees. Luckily, in February when I moved in, my neighbor Richard told me that these seemingly dead trees were indeed living fruit trees. Sure enough, in a week or two I saw signs of life and was told, by numerous tree kibbitzers, that my trees were in desperate need of pruning, but it was now too late in the season.

Luckily, though, it was not too late to start a garden. Now, I'm not the kind of a guy people usually think of as a gardener: I grew up more comfortable with books and art than with practical things like growing food. I like to tell people that reality is my weak suit. But having a garden was forced on me, many years ago, shortly after I moved into my old apartment. There was this narrow strip of land between our apartment and the house next door. This land got about two hours of sun a day, but even if it had received full sun I'd have never started a garden, except for the old lady next door, Mrs. Lima.

Mr. Lima was alive when we first moved in, conspicuous to us mainly for his morning spitting. But then he died, and of course we expressed our sympathies, and we suddenly felt obliged to sort of watch over Mrs. Lima. Really, though, she watched over us, encouraging our toddlers to play on her steps and giving us tours of her backyard, a backyard that turned out to be giant vegetable garden. A farm, in Berkeley!

We were naive about such things then, so my wife and I thought she was being incredibly generous when she started giving us almost daily zucchini. We didn't quite know what to do, that first summer, but my mother (long-distance) told us how to make zucchini parmesan, which soon became a dietary staple: "Sauté sliced zucchini in olive oil. Drain oil from frying pan; return all slices to pan. Cover zucchini with spaghetti sauce. Top with slices of mozzarella and cover. Simmer until mozzarella has melted."

Then Mrs. Lima started suggesting that we should really make our own garden out of the sunless rocky strip between our apartment and her house. I realized that she found overgrown weeds and barren land a personal affront, so to please her, I weeded and turned over the soil. Mrs. Lima was especially delighted when my wife came out to put seedlings in the ground. She suggested that somehow it was ritualistically appropriate for the woman to put the seed into the ground, and for the man to water it. Eventually, we harvested some scrawny tomatoes, a few leaves of lettuce, an occasional stalk of broccoli. Out of politeness, we never planted zucchini.

I loved that little garden, although it never produced much. I kept it going, year after year, even after Mrs. Lima died. We nurtured the calla lilies, planted poinsettias for the Christmas season, planted roses and more lilies when my third child (Lily) was born. We saved an avocado pit from guacamole and turned it into a tree, which grew like a beanstalk, taller than the building. The day my father died, I found an uprooted pine tree at a park and planted that, and it flourished too. I hated to leave that little garden. I was afraid no one else would care for such a small sunless spot.

But the new house had southern exposure in the backyard, and I soon had, with my friend Victor's help, raised bed gardens. And Richard frequently dropped by, almost conspiratorially offering me seedlings of spaghetti squash, corn, pumpkins, and, of course, zucchini. He told me how once he had tried, in Berkeley, to be entirely self-subsistent. He claimed to have been fairly successful in this admirable new-age adventure, but he abandoned the project when he discovered himself growing increasingly grouchy and, I guess, hungry. With age, he'd controlled his fanaticism a bit, but gardening was obviously still a religion (or an addiction) with him, and he was delighted to see me converted (or hooked).

So every day, spring and summer, I'd go out and watch the growth, the new life. For breakfast I picked pears or apples; I was outside every day, and I drank less, slept better, and lost weight. For the first time in my life, I could observe the gradual transformation of corn, could appreciate all the mythology around this plant. Garden tomatoes with fresh cucumbers and cilantro were a daily lunch. But the most amazing vegetable of all was the humble, but prodigious, prodigal, and profligate zucchini. Whole zucchinis formed overnight. I felt like I could actually see them grow.

Among gardeners, I discovered, there is a sort of zucchini war: you are in a competition to find the few who will take some zucchini. Of course, I wasn't hostile or foolish enough to try to give another gardener one of my zucchinis, but I did foist off a spaghetti squash on Victor's wife. I thought I was being nice, but I discovered that no zucchini gardener likes any kind of squash sent to his house. To make up for my inappropriate gift, I gave Victor my mother's recipe for zucchini parmesan (so easy, so good, so zucchini-effective). But Victor, a veteran gardener, retaliated: he invited us for dinner and served us zucchini parmesan—using my mother's recipe!

Of course I understood. There are no ethics when it comes to moving your zucchini. The whole point of baby zucchini is not that it tastes any better (does zucchini actually have any taste?), but rather than you go through your zucchini faster when you harvest the little ones. And I'm sure of the real motivation for Dr. Ruth's advice that women use zucchini to masturbate; she's really giving a gardening tip, not sex therapy. Anything to find another use for a zuke.

In August, I went on a camping trip with four other families. Each family had brought zucchini bread! We felt a real solidarity, each helping the other consume our zucchini—washed down by gimlets. After the weekend, I returned to the city to see how my garden—and zucchini—had grown.

The next day my mother died, and summer was over.

I flew back east that night, at the last minute picking some pink flowers from our little front-yard garden to place on my mother's coffin. It was an all-night flight, and I clutched my silly little flowers most of the way. I had to change planes in Dallas, and in the airport men's room, standing at a urinal peeing, holding my little pin flowers, I noticed this big Chicano guy looking at me with a grin on his face. "Hey, naked ladies," he said. I tried to look friendly, but not too friendly, my tired sad mind trying to decipher his meaning. He laughed and gestured at the flowers: "Yeah, I love naked ladies, too. They for your girlfriend?" Now I understood—"naked ladies" was the name of my little flowers. "Yeah, they're for my girlfriend," I said, not feeling like I was lying, suddenly loving this stranger who seemed to love me and my naked ladies.

Later in the week, when my wife and kids arrived for the funeral, they brought fresher flowers, and we threw them on the coffin at the grave site. When the grave was covered, there was only the bare ground, not even the comfort of grass over the dirt. There was a stone with my father's name, but we had to wait for my mother's name to be carved in. A neighbor of hers had told my nephew that my mother was life itself, and so we chose as an epitaph: "They were life itself." And they were, but now life was dead, as grass or flowers would never grow over that bare grave.

My wife and kids left, but I stayed and spent a couple of weeks with my sisters, dealing with my mother's stuff: giving away, putting away, sorting out. It's hard to give away stuff in suburban New Jersey—there are no free boxes, and Salvation Army won't send a truck to pick up stuff. Fortunately, one of my sisters called a Baptist church that seemed interested in the free stuff. At first, we were being charitable, and they were grateful. But as the days went on, and we showed up with carload after carload of bric-a-brac, lamps, books, food, rugs, etc., the situation reversed. They, like the neighbor who accepts your zucchini, were being charitable to us.

Finally my mother's apartment was almost as bare as her grave site, and I flew back home. I left at sunset, so, flying towards the sun, I watched the clouds at sunset for hours, changing shapes and colors, transforming, dying, disappearing, being reborn, and finally vanishing into darkness.

Back in Berkeley, the kids were getting ready for school. My fruit trees were pretty much done producing fruit. The corn was gone. The broccoli seedlings had all died. There were still tomatoes, and, of course, the zucchini kept coming, but I couldn't really care. Berkeley really just has two seasons anyway: spring/summer and winter/fall, and I was ready for winter.

There's a medieval (circa 1320) poem about winter I've always liked. It begins (my translation):

> Winter wakens all my care;
> Now these trees are growing bare.
> I often sigh and clutch my hair,
> When it comes into my thought
> That all this world's joy come to nought.

Winter's the time for death, for realizing that it all comes to nothing, for mourning in the wasteland. I loved it when the leaves fell off my fruit trees and the trees looked as dead as I felt. I mechanically started more broccoli and some beets for a winter crop, but the birds got them, or they just died, and I didn't really care. I drove by my old apartment and saw that my neighbors had never planted on the old strip, and indeed had cut down the avocado and the pine tree. I was mad but not surprised. The medieval winter poem ends:

> In graves we bury good green grain
> By some command it starts to wane.
> Sweet Jesus let us make some gain,
> And protect us please from hell;
> For where and when I'm going I just can't tell.

I was ready for everything to wane. With a little help from me, even the zucchini finally died.

After a few months, past the dead of winter but still before spring, I began pruning my trees. Of course, I had no idea how to prune, but, needing to cut away the deadwood and the undesirable growth, I bought *The Sunset Pruning Handbook* and set to work.

But the *Sunset* book hadn't prepared me for the almost addictive pleasure involved in cutting those wayward branches, shaping up those trees. My fruit trees seemed almost like dogs; they obviously liked discipline, would behave better and respect me more because of it.

I pruned with a vengeance. For a while, I couldn't look at any tree without imagining where I would cut it and how my benevolent aggression would help it. My wife understood nothing of this. Whenever she went outside, she'd see me ankle deep in branches and twigs. She'd say "Haven't you done enough?" or "Shouldn't you stop now?" or simply, "Stop it, stop it, stop it."

I think women have more natural sympathy for things with roots. One of the things I admire about my friend Richard is that he likes to move trees. His wife is always complaining that trees should stay put, but Richard has a vision of what his yard should be, and he keeps moving his trees around in an attempt to realize this vision. Indeed, early this February I went over to his yard to help him dig up a semidwarf apricot tree for me; he'd realized he needed a smaller apricot, so the tree wouldn't block the southern light through his window. It was clear that his wife, hidden somewhere in the inner recesses of the house, didn't like all this uprooting and replanting. "Maybe she figures that if I can get rid of a tree so easily, she could be next," he speculated as he cut the root ball. I took the tree home and planted it and, with my tender-hearted wife safely in the house, pruned it.

All this pruning was therapy for me. I began to look forward to the spring, but then my wife's father died, and I knew there was still some winter left. A few days after my wife came back from the east, I was out in my yard and noticed that one vegetable, chard, had flourished through the winter. Chard is really an everpurple, refusing to die, signifying, like the Christmas tree, that through winter and death, life goes on.

And now, every day, the buds and flowers are coming out more and more. No matter what, spring does come: I'd better start germinating seeds. Soon it will be time to plant. I'll spend the summer eating fruits and vegetables. I'll find myself in the zucchini wars, preoccupied with this not very nutritious, not very delicious vegetable, OD'ing on zucchini parmesan, marveling at nature's capacity to create life and even too much life out of what's buried in the ground.

Some friends of mine have a marvelous poster with a line from the poet Pablo Neruda: "I'd like to do to you what Spring does to the cherry trees." But this beautiful and erotic line doesn't say what I really feel: I'd like Spring to do to me what it does to the fruit trees. After the dormancy of winter, and a year of dealing with deaths and burials, the seedlings emerge from the earth, the seemingly dead fruit trees start to bud and blossom with life. I'd like to blossom, too. I'm done with death. There's nothing more to bury, except seeds. I'm done with pruning trees. There's nothing more to do, except wait for the fruit.

Notes: My Mother at the Piano

FOR YEARS, WHEN I'D SIT DOWN to play the piano, I'd often get a funny feeling of almost remembering something. I'd try to let it come, to see what my mind had, over there, hidden in the corner, off to the side. But when I'd try to look, it would be gone; when I'd try to listen, it would fade away. So I'd forget it and begin to play. I was regularly haunted by this lost memory, but I recently discovered what it was.

My mother's mother, my Grandma Schneider, once started taking secret piano lessons in order to surprise her husband, who loved music—he sometimes went to German beer gardens in St. Louis and sang with the band or took over the conducting. Grandma knew Grandpa would be pleased if she learned to play the piano, so she started lessons, practicing when he was out of the house, at work. But one day, before she had progressed very far, he came home early and heard her practicing. Her surprise was ruined, so she gave up the lessons and never played again.

Grandma Schneider, a German immigrant and former housemaid, encouraged her children to be musical. She used to give my mother, Margaret Schneider, the choice of cleaning her room or practicing the piano. I guess my mother practiced the piano a lot; throughout her life, she never was very neat.

One of her piano teachers was a nun, who would hit her on the hands with a ruler when she made a mistake or when she didn't cup her hands sufficiently. My mother always had very good technique.

As a teenager, she used to practice the piano and typing on the bus, silently playing Rachmaninoff or "The Quick Brown Fox" on her lap over and over until she got to her stop. The skills of typing and piano playing are related—both develop and require finger coordination and strength. My mother had, as I do, these large piano-player hands (good for basketball and rock climbing, too, I've found). As a small child, though, my mother had had the tip of the index finger on her left hand cut off when, playing hide-and-go-seek with her father, she caught her finger in the falling top of a rolltop desk. Her sister, a gifted classical pianist, feels that this accident kept Margaret from really developing as a classical musician, that this accident led her to more popular music. It was also the tip of this finger being gone that allowed me to recognize her bloated and strange body after her death, to make the ID required by law.

She studied classical piano and was musically gifted (learning the cello in her spare time when a nun informed her the St. Louis Youth symphony needed a cello player), but she really took to popular music. Her first marriage was to a jazz drummer, a relatively despicable man as far as I can tell. Shortly before her death, one of her grown-up granddaughters asked why she had married this eccentric, obnoxious man. "I was a shithead," my mother explained succinctly.

Part of the attraction, though, was no doubt his drumming: the piano player and the drummer making beautiful music together.

Musicians, like most artists, don't make much money. So the marriage with the drummer, despite two kids, was soon on the rocks ("When money goes out the door, love goes out the window," Mom used to say). My mother took a night job playing the piano at a speakeasy. My mother always played great party piano. She knew more songs than anybody and could fake anything—if you'd hum a few bars, she'd play it. She was also beautiful, very thin and tall, with savage black hair and strikingly high cheek bones (as an old woman, she said of her earlier beauty: "When I needed it I had it, now I don't need it and I don't have it"). I can't imagine a better piano player for a speakeasy.

One night at the speakeasy, a World War I vet came in. He had this steel plate in his head. Because of the plate, he wasn't supposed to drink but, of course, being in a speakeasy he knocked back a couple of drinks. Then he decided to tear the place apart. It became a classic bar fight, bottles breaking, chairs thrown. My mother hid under the bar. Also under the bar was a salesman, hat in hand, the man who would become my father. Meeting this attractive woman under a bar during a bar fight he did, I suppose, the natural thing: he grabbed a bottle and poured them both drinks.

Until my mother was an old lady and the doctor suggested it for her high blood pressure, she never drank at all. She'd play the piano through many a party but never have a drink. Maybe she remembered the dramatic changes that could come from a drink, like the time at the speakeasy when she took the first step toward a second marriage and consequent excommunication.

My mother divorced the drummer but, freaked out from having been poor, refused to marry my father until he had $500 in the bank. Finally, my father said he had the money, and so they got married. Unfortunately, he actually owed $500 at the time, but he never worried about money and ended up making a lot of it. He never would allow my mother to work though, maybe remembering that he met her when she was working. And so my mother, before, during, and after having three more kids with my father (making us a family of seven), became a volunteer or amateur piano player. She refused any jobs playing the piano if they required her to take money.

My earliest nighttime memories are the sounds of the party downstairs, the sounds of singing around the piano: Risqué songs like "Twelve Old Ladies Locked in the Lavatory" ("They were there from Monday to Saturday / Nobody knew they were there"), with the obligatory twelve verses about various old women named Elizabeth, such as Elizabeth Wren (who got the wrong door and had to stand in line with the men) and Elizabeth Crandall (who suffered the indignity of sitting on the handle). Sad songs about old hometowns (like the poignant "Southie," which some guy from Boston would always request). Songs with bawdy lyrics it took me a few years to get ("When roses are red they're ready for pluckin' / And girls of sixteen are ready for high school"). Holy roller songs like "The Joy" (first stanza: "I got the Joy Joy Joy Joy down in my heart, down in my heart, down in my heart / I got the Joy Joy Joy Joy down in my heart / Jesus is keepin' me alive"; Second stanza: "The holy ghost, the ball of fire, keepin' me alive"; third stanza: "Oh it's all over [fill in name] and it's keepin' him alive"). The popular songs of all eras. The song games, with improvised lyrics; taking phone numbers and making them into songs. My mother had a trick of taking a well-known song and changing it slightly (playing it real slow, putting in 3/4, shifting it into a minor key, for example), so that you could almost recognize it but not quite; then when you did recognize it, you'd feel that "Oh, of course" epiphany. My father, with his astounding memory for lyrics, loud (although not always on key) voice, and large capacity for liquor was the leader at these song sessions, which would go on and on long after I'd fallen to sleep upstairs, the twelve old ladies dancing in my dreams.

"The Twelve Old Ladies" actually led me to my first conscious lie, I suppose to my beginnings as a storyteller. We were living in L.A., and I was in kindergarten. The teacher decided as part of Show and Tell that everyone would sing a song. We sat in a circle and each of us in turn stood up to sing. What would I sing? The only songs I really knew were "The Joy" and "Twelve Old Ladies Locked in the Lavatory." I knew from the other kids' songs ("Mary Had a Little Lamb," "Mairzy Dotes," "Oh, My Darling Clementine") that mine wouldn't fit in, so on my turn I copied some other kid and did "Mary Had a Little Lamb."

When I got home, I told my mother about that day's Show and Tell, "Yeah, Mom, I sang 'The Joy' for them," I lied, not quite knowing why I was lying but loving my mother's combined horror and amusement, "and they all liked that so much I sang 'Twelve Old Ladies Locked in the Lavatory,' but Miss Duncan wouldn't let me sing all of it. I guess it was too long." My mother gasped, her eyes opened wide, but she laughed. "Wait till I tell your father." I was pleased with myself and never revealed the truth.

When I was little, my mother used to give me sheets of music paper. I'd sit on the floor and draw circles, filling some of the circles in, putting staffs on various of the notes, connecting some of the staffs. When I'd finish, my mother would play my compositions—intuiting the divisions between bars. These songs, played with full arrangement, chords and all, were usually beautiful to my ears. If she or I didn't particularly like one of these songs, she'd turn the sheet of music upside down and play it again (John Cage would have been proud). One way or another, either upside down or right side up, I'd have composed a lovely song.

The only problem with my love for music was that I seem to have inherited my father's musical abilities and was pretty much tone deaf. My mother, though, in her own undisciplined way, educated my ear. When we drove somewhere, she would kill the time by singing notes, starting with one very high, one very low. Then she'd ask me which was higher. At first, I usually couldn't tell, but soon through this automotive ear training I began to notice differences in pitch, and she correspondingly brought the notes closer and closer together.

She didn't force piano lessons on any of her kids, but she exposed us to them. My sister Margaret—who remembers nights of wishing she could go to sleep and wake up in the morning and magically be able to play as well as Mom—persevered with them for years, becoming a real piano player. But after only a few months of torture, my sister Karen and I decided to quit. Unlike Karen, I wanted to quit in person. I dutifully showed up at my lesson, not having practiced at all during the week, had my piano teacher scold me, then at the end of the lesson, told her to her face that I quit. I've quit many things since then (mostly jobs) and always, like this first time, found the experience exhilarating.

When we'd visit my mother's parents in St. Louis, I'd always end up playing the piano, perhaps because the only toys in the house were numerous decks of cards and one set of ivory dominos. But there was something fascinating about that beautiful black baby grand with the framed picture of my mother at nineteen sitting on it (the same picture now sits on my piano). So, bored with nothing else to do, I would fiddle on the piano. But all I knew how to play were the three notes of a major chord—so I'd put on the loud pedal and play those three notes over and over, rippling them together in a shower of sound, a blurry cascade, and my grandma would always come into the room and tell me how nice it sounded. She said it so genuinely that I'd think, "Yes, it really does sound nice."

By the time I was in high school, my older brother, a jazz fan, had taught me how to play open sevenths with the left hand and fiddle around with any notes at all with the right, so that the result sounded vaguely like jazz piano. This new ability to make jazzy sounds on the piano inspired me to try lessons again. I really learned to play, at age 16 or so, in six months of lessons from a guy who'd studied piano with John Lewis (of the Modern Jazz Quartet). He taught me the secret of how to play from chords, so that I could read music without having to read all those damn notes in the left hand, so that I could start to improvise by playing around with notes in the chords. But after these six months of lessons, my mother was my only teacher, although she never sat down to give me a lesson. I have hundreds of memories of sitting at the piano, playing something and hearing her voice from the kitchen, full of pain at my dissonant mistake but full of love, too—"B-flat! B-flat!"

During those high school years, she used to play the piano regularly for the mental patients at Bergen Pines Hospital. Once a patient snuck up behind her when she was playing and dropped his false teeth down the back of her dress. Another time a woman started screaming at her when she was playing Mozart. "That's not right! That's not right!" the woman kept shouting, growing more and more upset, until the orderlies dragged her away to sedate and restrain her. My mother felt guilty about this, for she knew the complaining woman had been right. My mother had been playing a Mozart sonata from memory, a piece she *had* known years before, but she was now, in her fashion, faking it, playing mostly Mozart, but clearly not playing it right.

At the mental hospital, sometimes she'd accompany a woman who sang opera music. I don't remember her name, but I do recall that she was the actor Adolph Menjou's sister. My mother was a great accompanist, used to slowing down or speeding up as singers capriciously changed their tempo, but this woman had the especially annoying habit of changing keys in the middle of a piece. After a long rest, when the woman was supposed to come in *a cappella*, she would come in with her long, high, beautiful but wrong note, and it would put the piece in a whole new key. My mother would complain at home, but at the mental ward she'd just change keys and keep playing.

In high school, summers and weekends, I got into the habit of sleeping late. When my mother thought I'd slept long enough, she'd start playing the piano, each song louder and faster than the previous one, on into barrelhouse and boogie woogie and I'd wake up to the sound of music. When, later in life, I visited her, she still woke me up with her piano playing (sometimes because it was time for us to go to garage sales). Her piano playing was the best alarm clock ever invented.

There was a time when my parents stopped having their all night singing parties and we kids started having them. My sister Margaret would play the piano (I wasn't good enough for a singalong yet), and we'd sing the good old songs, "My Buddy," "Ready for the

River," "Ragged But Right," "Put the Blame on Mame"), Tin Pan Alley songs from George M. Cohan to Cole Porter, and the new songs of the day (Beatles, "Abraham, Martin and John," "You're So Vain"). My mother had this huge collection of sheet music, to which we added.

There'd come a time, usually around two in the morning, when we were just going good, that my mother would come down the stairs in her slip and plead for us to keep it down, "or else your father will be up making coffee." I guess it was karma or just our turn, but it didn't feel like sweet revenge—they hadn't wanted to keep us up with their singing any more than we wanted to keep them up. We just wanted to sing, so we'd keep singing but with the soft pedal on, or sometimes we'd break up the party and go to bed, or sometimes we'd get loud again and in a few minutes my father would come down the stairs in his polkadot boxer shorts and old-fashioned t-shirt and start making coffee. He never seemed to mind having been wakened; it was my mother who couldn't stand the idea of his waking up this early, starting his day when his kids were still at the end of the night. We'd sing a few more songs, then to the smell of coffee brewing say goodnight and go upstairs, leaving my father to read his morning through.

Once she showed me this beautiful slightly dissonant but full rich chord. It was at least eight notes, played with both hands, then as you'd descend a half step at a time down the scale, the chord would resonate, hauntingly. I played it for a few weeks when I'd sit down to fiddle at the piano. Then I stopped playing it, forgot about it. One day years later I remembered and asked my mother to show me this haunting chord again. What chord? she said, I never showed you such a chord. The Lost Chord died with my mother, indeed died before she did.

One of the distinctive features of her piano style was how much she loved the low notes. She would stride down to the very bottom of the piano with her left hand, making a full deep bass sound for the melody on top. Now when I play I still try to learn from her, not to dwell too long or too much in the easy middle.

I was always shocked by how little she liked to listen to music. She appreciated it—hell, she could always tell just where in the melody the jazz soloist was — but she always felt that if she wanted music she would play it, not listen to it.

As a writer I can identify with this attitude. I once heard Raymond Carver say that writers were people who wrote little books of their own instead of reading other people's big books. Of course, you appreciate other people's art, but the main thing is to do it yourself, to play your instrument, to make your music. I used to read all the time, with music in the background. Now more and more I write, I play the piano.

Shortly before she died, we went to her friend Vivian's house for dinner. Vivian was still dressing upstairs, so my mother, my wife, and my kids, sat in her luxurious living room while I helped myself to Vivian's piano. I played for a few minutes until I heard Vivian descending the stairs. "You know," my mother said to me, "You play the piano very well." These words were as sincere as her own mother's compliments had been (and indeed I had become a good piano player). Her praise not only made my night, it made the rest of my life.

One Monday when she was seventy-five she had heart surgery, and I sat on the opposite coast waiting for the phone call and playing the piano. I played out of one of the many fake books she had given me (fake books are books with the melody and chords for hundreds of songs; when the writers of the songs are given no royalties, such books are illegal, but nonetheless invaluable to musicians; my mother bought several of them in the late fifties for $25.00 each). I played over and over the sweet sad song "I'll Never Be the Same" ("I'll never be the same / Stars have lost their meaning to me / And when the songbirds that sing / Tell me it's spring / I can't believe their song / I'll never be the same / Again"). When I got the call that she had died on the operating table, this became the last song I would associate with her.

One of my strongest ways of remembering her is by remembering and playing the songs she especially liked. Old songs like "Do You Know What It Means to Miss New Orleans" and "Mean to Me," obscure jazz tunes like Russ Freeman's "Happy Little Sunbeam" and Lennie Niehaus's "Whose Blues," classical music by Brahms. Once in the seventies she mentioned how much she liked John Lennon's song "Imagine." Ah yes, I sympathized, glad that she'd finally come around to the movement, what wonderful sentiments in those lyrics, "Imagine all the people . . . ." But she cut me off: "What lyrics? I just think the tune is nice."

When my sisters and I attended Ridgewood High School in New Jersey, my mother began playing piano for Jamboree, an annual fund-raising musical show the Ridgewood High parents and teachers put on each year. After we had all graduated, she kept being asked back to be the piano player, logging 1,300 hours at rehearsals and shows. She also acted as song finder—finding melodies in her sheet music collection for which new lyrics could be written. After her death, one of the Jamboree producers wrote a little eulogy in which she referred to "shy Margaret, hiding behind the drummer."

Like many introverts, she could seem loud and even boisterous to those she met in a small group. But she didn't want to be the center of attention. She was the perfect accompanist—preferring to have herself unseen and her music heard, hiding behind the drummer (I think of her first husband, the drummer).

For her, music was a social act. Late in life, when she had arthritis in her fingers, she practiced regularly, not so much for the pleasure of playing, but so that she could continue to play for people. She liked to play for parties, for friends, children, and grandchildren (one set of grandkids always requested her rendition of Mezz Mezrow's "Kitten on the Keys"), for dancing schools, for shows big and little, for churches and for synagogues, for people. After playing, her music was, of course, gone forever, a momentary gift that brightened life but couldn't last, a genuine spiritual act.

The painter J. B. Yeats (the poet's father) called art the social act of the solitary man. When I'm at a party and there's a piano, I understand what J. B. Yeats meant, I understand how my mother must have felt, I understand the desirability of getting to hide behind music, to hide behind the piano, to not have to mix and seek people out, but to still be contributing, really contributing to the feeling of the party.

Whenever I see a strange piano, I want to touch it, to play it. The piano in any room calls to me, like an attractive and willing woman who wants me to love her, to play with her. Freud would probably say this feeling has something to do with my mother complex, with how I associate my mother (my first image of the feminine) with the piano.

When I finally recovered my lost memory, the memory that sometimes tried to come up when I sat down alone in a quiet room at the piano, I was amazed I hadn't figured it out before. I was trying to recall what is undoubtedly my first memory: the sound of piano music. Here I am, *inside* my mother and I hear this wonderful stuff—piano music. There I am, in my cradle, and I hear strange but beautiful sounds. What are they? What is it? It's my mother at the piano.

Life Itself

My mother, born in 1911, was a teenager when the twenties roared: she responded to the call and became a flapper. (It's no wonder that, a generation later, I similarly rose to the bait of the sixties and became a hippie.) Her favorite flapper item of jewelry was a live chameleon. The chameleon had a collar and chain around its neck, and she could pin it to whatever dress she was wearing. Her lizard would shade its color to match whatever my mother was wearing. Whenever she'd tell me this story, I'd imagine the shock of her date noticing that the chameleon pin on her chest was moving, was alive.

She had many boyfriends, not all of them denizens of the moral high ground. When she was fourteen, her first real boyfriend, Norman Kruppelvitch, gave her a garnet and pearl ring, which he had stolen from his older sister. My daughter Amy still wears that ring.

My mother didn't tell me traditional nursery tales; rather she told stories of her flapper days. I especially loved to hear about St. Louis's most bizarre criminal, "the Feets Burglar." Summers in St. Louis were unbearably hot, so everyone slept with their windows open. This one summer, a young man, wearing only his underwear, began sneaking in the windows of bedrooms where young women were sleeping. He would creep up to their beds and tickle their feet until they woke up. The women would, of course, scream at the sight of a strange man in his underwear tickling their feet, and he would then disappear out the window. The newspapers named this summertime intruder "the Feets Burglar." The Feets Burglar became the talk of the town that summer, a summer when my mother had a steady boyfriend named Freddy ("a very nice boy," my mother always added). Imagine my mother's surprise when one August morning she opened the paper to find that the Feets Burglar had finally been apprehended, and it was Freddy. Her steady boyfriend had been the Feets Burglar!

Friday night was the big party night. My mother and her girlfriend Marge (both good Catholics) would look in the paper to see where there was a wake being held, then they would crash it. They'd go into the living room, look at the body, commiserate with the weeping women, then head to the kitchen where the men would be drinking and the party would be getting down. Wakes made for excellent parties, she always assured me.

My mother frequently gave me two pieces of advice joined into one sentence: "Don't be the first one home from the party and don't worry about your grades." Ironically, I turned out to be motivated in school (I ended with a Ph.D.), but I never worried about my grades as much as others seemed to worry about theirs, and I have never been the first one home from any good party.

Throughout my childhood, whenever I left the house she would kiss me goodbye at the door and then add, "And remember to keep your big mouth shut." Actually, this advice served as much to remind me that I had a big mouth as to remind me to keep it shut.

My mother was not a loud person, but she attracted (even encouraged) loudness and laughter. Just as she was the perfect party piano player, creating a mood for others to be the lives of the party, she was the perfect social companion, creating a mood for others (such as myself) to come to life. Many's the time I was at a restaurant with my mother and the conversational hysterics got out of hand so that she became embarrassed, even angry, that we were too noisy, laughing too loud. I always slightly surprised because I'd feel that she was really the cause of it all.

Once my wife and I and our three daughters were out to dinner with her at a fancy restaurant, when my two-year-old, Lily, needed to go to the bathroom. I offered to take her to the men's room. My mother was aghast.

"You can't take her in the men's room," she insisted.

"Hey," I protested, in my modern mode, "when I was little you used to take me to the ladies' room."

"That's totally different," my mother maintained. "In the men's room, there are all these men in there waving their things and going 'ho ho ho.' " The conversation soon degenerated into an increasingly boisterous discussion of men's rooms and then of urinal cakes—like many women, my mother didn't know what a urinal cake was—

until finally, amid laughter turning to tears, she had to adopt her serious tone and tell us all to quiet down. "Ho, ho, ho," I replied.

When we moved to New Jersey, in the summer of 1956, I didn't have much to do, so I went shopping with my mother at the A & P. I was at first somewhat embarrassed to find her regularly doing therapy (although I didn't know that word yet) for strangers in the checkout line. Throughout her life, people asked her advice. One of her secrets as a lay therapist was that she gave her honest responses; she wasn't California noncommittal, with the "What do you think, how do you feel about that" approach. I remember hearing one young woman detail her problems with a boyfriend. My mother listened intently, then told the girl, "Dump him."

I think she became so sure of herself because my father traveled regularly throughout their married life. When I was a child, I usually didn't know whether he was in Pittsburgh, at work, or just upstairs sleeping; we just didn't see him that often. Thus my mother became independent, self-sufficient. When my father died, my mother grieved, of course, but she was after all pretty much used to living alone. She liked it.

Every year for the last twenty-one, I have gone backpacking for a week with three men friends. When my mother was alive, she'd always call my wife after I'd left and say, "Isn't it great to have him gone!" She believed that men and women should enjoy being able to take care of themselves, to have their own friends, live their own lives.

Late in life, she began using a variant of "Don't be the first one home from the party," telling any young person who wanted to stay up late and/or had to get up early: "Don't worry, you can always sleep while you're old." But when she was old (in fact, throughout her life) she hardly slept at all. She loved life, and I don't think she could ever understand how someone like me could seem to prefer sleep to living. She'd listen to talk radio all night long, not wanting to waste life in silent darkness. When a certain set of young grandkids would visit, they'd sneak into her bedroom when it was still dark and tickle her feet, and (amazing!) she would wake up laughing.

She was a great mother. On cold winter mornings, when I was little, she would warm my socks and underwear on the radiator before waking me up by slipping warm socks on my feet. And she always had new jokes, dirty ones and clean ones. When I was a young boy, she made me promise that if I ever heard a dirty joke with the punchline, "Not tonight Josephine," to tell it to her. She had heard the joke once, thought it was tremendously funny, but had uncharacteristically forgotten the set-up. This task, of course, gave me maternal encouragement to spend a lifetime listening to dirty jokes, but I am sad to say I never did hear the "Not tonight, Josephine" one.

She was a great cook—to my wife and me, her most valuable heirloom was her recipe file. After she died, my sisters and I spent weeks cleaning out her apartment; one evening we defrosted some frozen enchiladas she had made. Eating her food after she was dead was poignant—mother still feeding us—enchiladas salted with tears—but it was also just good food, no doubt the best enchiladas being eaten in New Jersey that evening.

After dinner, the doorbell rang. It was a neighbor offering condolences. This woman hadn't known my mother particularly well, but she summed her up for us, saying with a shrug, "She was life itself."